YOUR WINNING EDGE

God's Power Perfected in Weakness

A Six-week Personal Growth Journey

ENDORSEMENTS

This book is life changing—the cutting edge to win in a high-pressure world. Candidly sharing their personal struggles, Pastor Dave and Joanne communicate insights for turning weakness into strength. Filled with clear teaching from God's Word, they connect truth for life's ups and downs.

—John Thune, United States Senator

Your Winning Edge has the backbone of real insight for life change that only comes from forty-plus years of ministry. Dave and Joanne have put together a study that offers hope and change for those places we all struggle. So many of us have a sense that there is a victorious life of faith that seems just out of our reach. Through the reading, individual exercises, and small group discussion this study will show you how God brings that life of promise within your grasp.

—Tom Holladay, Teaching Pastor, Saddleback Church, Lake Forest, California

This book is the best Bible study I have read that explains how to live the Christian life. The book is full of examples that demonstrate the power of living out the teachings of Jesus. It describes how to apply Biblical teaching in practical and useful ways that will impact your life and those around you.

—Craig Kitchens, Movie Producer and President, Hometown Studio and Distribution

The church today is in dire need of Bible study material that not only informs the mind with truth but equally targets to transform the heart. *Your Winning Edge* by Dave and Joanne Beckwith scores the highest marks on both accounts. Each chapter is biblically insightful, the exercises personally practical, and the group discussions designed to cultivate authentic believer community. This book is life transforming.

—**Pastor Lou Damiani**, Church Discipleship Ministries, The Navigators

Dave was a leader ... starting in his student days at Biola University and Talbot Seminary. His love for God's Word and desire to share Christ were evident as a pastor, conference director, and mission's leader. Dave and Joanne's life theme is "God's awesome power displayed in our weakness." I guarantee you'll be blessed by this book.

—**Ron Hafer**, Chaplain (Retired), Biola University

Your Winning Edge is must reading for the pastor, missionary and para-church leader couples we minister to.

—**Dr. Rex and Eve Johnson**, Marriage and Family Counselors, Talbot School of Theology (retired), Standing Stone Shepherds, author of seven books

I have enjoyed friendship and in-depth spiritual conversation with Dave and Joanne Beckwith for over thirty years. Their insights always open my eyes to see God more clearly and love him more dearly. As you delve into their writings, I know you will be greatly blessed and deeply challenged in very practical ways to grow in your walk with God.

—**Kitty Jones**, Women's Bible Study Author and Teacher

We all have weaknesses and shortcomings in our lives that unless addressed can undermine our efforts and sabotage our success. Based on their personal life experiences and the solid teaching of Scripture, Dave and Joanne Beckwith present a practical plan for helping us face our flaws and turn our liabilities into assets. If you are serious about making real changes in your life, this book is for you.

—**Dr. Gary Tangeman**, Lead Pastor, Celebration Church, Santa Ana, California

YOUR WINNING EDGE

God's Power Perfected in Weakness

A SIX-WEEK PERSONAL GROWTH JOURNEY

Dave and Joanne Beckwith

PUBLISHING THE POSITIVE

ELK LAKE PUBLISHING INC
Plymouth, Massachusetts

The authors are represented by WordWise Media Services

Cover and graphics design: Derinda Babcock

Editing: Jerry Gramckow, Kathi Macias, Judy Hagey, Deb Haggerty

PUBLISHED BY: Elk Lake Publishing, Inc., Plymouth, MA 02360, 2019

Library Cataloging Data

Names: Beckwith, Dave and Joanne (Dave and Joanne Beckwith)

Your Winning Edge: God's Power Perfected in Weakness/Dave and Joanne Beckwith

308 p. 23cm × 15cm (9in × 6 in.)

Description: Sharpen your edge in life as you discover how God perfects his power in your inadequacies, failures, and frailties. Pretending to be strong is a great weakness--humbly acknowledging weakness is a great strength. God promises that his power works best in your weakness (2 Cor. 12:9). Discover how to exchange weakness for strength, defuse tormentors in the mind, release resentments and regrets, and deepen relationships.

Identifiers: ISBN 13: 978-1-951080-73-0 (Trade) | 978-1-951080-74-7 (POD) | 978-1-951080-75-4 (e-book)

Key Words: Strength, weakness, mind, mental tormentors, change, transformation, resentments, regrets, love

LCCN: 2019952684 Nonfiction

To our daughters:

Julie McGough
and
Tami Baker

Travelers with us in many of our life adventures
and eyewitnesses to our weaknesses.
You are both lovely, godly women who bring us much joy.
We thank God for you, and your love, encouragement,
and support.

TABLE OF CONTENTS

PREFACE

This book is about change and the edge we are given when God changes us. Change isn't always easy or fun but is necessary to help us become the men and women God wants us to be. The purpose of *Your Winning Edge* is to unlock the principles for life transformation through discovering God's strength in human weakness.

In a world where we are being told "only the strong survive," Dave and Joanne Beckwith give us a refreshing paradigm shift by going against the flow and reminding us of God's promise: "He gives power to the weak and strength to the powerless" (Is. 40:29 NLT). Using the life lessons they've learned through their many years of ministry, marriage, and living, Dave and Joanne give a practical guide to gain an edge in our lives by allowing the Lord to refine us by using our weaknesses. In the times of our darkest hours, our worst failures, and our greatest struggles, the Lord is refining us. This book will give us insights that can help us:

- Release resentments and regrets
- Control negative thought patterns
- Learn how to grow from our weaknesses
- Stop being intimidated and become God-empowered
- Learn the ABC's to free others to change

If you want to gain an edge on life by allowing the Lord to make some positive changes, do yourself a favor and begin reading and applying what you are about to learn from this book. You'll be glad you did!

—**Jim and Debbie Hogan,** Co-Founders of Standing Stone Ministry**,** authors of *Shepherding Shepherds: The Standing Stone Story*

INTRODUCTION:

A SIX-WEEK PERSONAL GROWTH JOURNEY

What would you like to happen in the next six weeks or forty days? Are there areas in your life that need transformation? Would you like to experience more of the power of God in the struggles of daily living? This forty-day personal growth journey is written to provide insights for deepening your walk with God and experiencing his power in new ways.

God has done some amazing things in forty days. He gave Moses the Ten Commandments during forty days on Mt. Sinai (Ex. 24:18). Elijah traveled forty days to Mt. Sinai where he had a life-changing encounter with God (1 Kings 19:8). Jonah preached for forty days and the great city of Nineveh repented (Jon. 3:4). Jesus fasted for forty days and nights before the start of his public ministry (Matt. 4:2). After his death and resurrection, Jesus showed himself alive for forty days, appearing to more than five hundred before his ascension into heaven (Acts 1:3).

What will God do in your life in the next forty days? This book is designed as a forty-day, six-week personal growth journey—a unique opportunity to discover God's power through your weaknesses. You will discover most weaknesses have a hidden, camouflaged strength—the perfectionist has the potential to be productive as well as thorough; those who grieve can develop a unique capacity to give comfort; and the reckless renegade can become a courageous champion for what is right.

Different than STRENGTHS FINDER, the popular Gallup assessment to discover your natural abilities and aptitudes, this is STRENGTHS BUILDER—God's power in human weakness that confounds the wisdom of the world and the power of the elite. "Human strength can't begin to compete with God's 'weakness.' Take a good look, friends, at who you were when you got called into this life. I don't see many of 'the brightest and the best' among you, not many influential, not many from high-society families. Isn't it obvious that God deliberately chose men and women that the culture overlooks and exploits and abuses, chose these 'nobodies' to expose the hollow pretensions of the 'somebodies'?" (1 Cor. 1:25-28 MSG).

This is hope for the disillusioned and disappointed, the so-called nobodies. Take heart. God displays his power in weakness. The deeply wounded are shaped into healers, the discarded become lifters of the downtrodden, the greedy become givers, and rebels become godly leaders.

Marriages, as well as friendships, grow deeper with an understanding of strengths and weaknesses. In relationships, opposites attract, but they also "rub," creating an agenda to change the other person. Is it possible to change someone you love? No. Changing a life is God's business, but you can be used by God to help someone change by cooperating with God's work in their life and becoming a STRENGTHS BUILDER.

This book is designed for reading one chapter each week; however, proceed at your own pace. A meditation verse is included for each week. Carry a copy of the verse with you, direct your thoughts to the words frequently throughout the day, and memorize it for maximum benefit. The chapters also include five daily "Time Outs" for your personal quiet time. Each day, read a short section until you come to the "Time Out." Stop there, read the Scripture included, seek the Lord in prayer, and apply what you've read.

Ask a few friends to join you as you read, and you'll have a "Time Together" for interaction, support, and encouragement. Each chapter includes materials for a small group. This is the "Time Together" guide, and each lesson includes five sections designed for healthy group life: Connect, Grow, Apply, Pray, and Share.

For clarification as you read, the chapters are primarily written by Dave unless noted otherwise. Joanne took the lead in writing the "Time Outs" and the "Time Together" materials for small groups.

Our heartfelt thanks to those who have encouraged us on the journey and provided wise counsel. Authors and freelance editors Kathi Macias and Kathi Ide taught the first all-day writing workshop I attended seven years ago. I thought I was a decent writer until they helped me see how much I had to learn. To have Kathi Macias as one of the editors of this book has been a privilege. She is an award-winning writer who has authored more than fifty books and ghostwritten several others. Friend to friend, she has given gentle correction and frequent encouragement. Steve Hutson, Literary Agent with WordWise Media, worked diligently to find the right publisher while providing frequent encouragement and guidance. Editor Jerry Gramckow provided his incredible scrutiny regarding the structure and grammar. I have learned a great deal from Judy Hagey who did the final editing. Deb Haggerty, publisher and editor-in-chief at Elk Lake Publishing, Inc., put the finishing touches on the book. I am also grateful to the team leading Orange County Christian Writers (now called Southern California Christian Writers Conference) who have provided a yearly conference with speakers and workshops where I have learned so much. Rich and Karen Thune, Maria Martinez, Lou Damiani, and others have helped out by reading and editing selected sections. Our thanks to Woodbridge Community Church for providing a test group for the small group materials. And a big thank you to our tech-savvy grandson, Sean McGough, who has repeatedly rescued us when we were ready to throw our computers off a cliff.

Just before this book went to print, Don Klassen, whose story is at the end of chapter two, passed from this life into the presence of the Lord. We're glad we could include his story as a testimony to his life. Our compassion and love to Sharon, his wonderful wife.

Enjoy discovering your winning edge ... turning weakness to strength. We pray God will give you his strength to overcome and live in joy and peace.

—Pastor Dave and Joanne Beckwith

CHAPTER ZERO:

THE EDGE …

… the cutting side of a blade,
… the threshold of danger or ruin,
… vigor and energy,
… keenness and intensity of desire,
… a favorable margin,
… an advantage.[1]

Welcome to "the edge." I live here. Teetering on the precipice, always a step from danger. Frequently tired and weak, I wait on God to renew my strength.

My struggle has always been that wherever I go, *there I am.* I polished the art of blaming others, but when my excuses ran out, I had to look in the mirror and admit—I was the problem. As someone observed, "If I could kick my worst enemy in the seat of the pants, I wouldn't be able to sit down for a week." That's me.

I was always hoping others would applaud my strengths. Some did but not for long. My weaknesses—faults, flaws, and inadequacies—were like the "sharp edge of a blade," cutting into my fragile sense of worth, leaving me disappointed, wounded, and bleeding. No, I was never a drug user, compulsive gambler, hatemonger, inside-trader, or murderer. Instead, manipulating

---

1. *Merriam-Webster's Dictionary and Thesaurus*, 20th Edition 2014, s.v. "edge."

and conniving to get my way, gluttony, resentment, hypocrisy, self-centeredness, out-of-control compulsiveness, and perfectionism derailed me over-and-over again. I lived with nagging self-disappointment.

Unchecked, my weaknesses could have led me to "the edge of ruin." I have often wondered what my life would be like if I hadn't been turned around by God. I surmise I'd be working in the business world, married three or four times, addicted to who knows what, having children who wouldn't talk to me, and burned out on life—that is, if I were still alive. A greater likelihood is that I would have died in my fifties like my father and grandfather.

Through the process of experiencing brokenness and discovering the power of Christ in my weaknesses, my life today is filled with the "cutting edge" of vigor and energy and "the sharpened edge" of intense desire. My weaknesses have become "power points" to the glory of God.

Weaknesses empowered by God are a winning edge, a distinct advantage. Paul, a radically reshaped man, leveraged his weaknesses to rise above life's obstacles. Paul discovered the power edge—the favorable margin to overcome seemingly insurmountable obstacles. His life-changing insight: "When I am weak, then I am strong" (2 Cor. 12:10).

When facing discouragement or feeling beat up with woundedness, discovering hidden strength in your weakness will give you fresh hope. It is a new way of living, a moment-by-moment God-dependence. Without him in control, failure is certain. God designed us with weaknesses, so we'd rely totally on him. This is *Your Winning Edge*.

—Dave Beckwith

CHAPTER ONE:

HEAD-ON WITH LIFE

I was trying to do it myself—while God was trying to bring me to the end of myself.

With the shrill sound of sirens, the smell of burning fuel, and flames piercing through the black darkness, I regained consciousness. Where was I? What was going on? Slowly I realized I was lying in the middle of the freeway. Then I remembered the two headlights coming straight at me! As I drifted in and out of consciousness, I heard my wife's voice, calm in assurance and deep in faith, reciting Psalm 23. "The LORD is my shepherd, … even though I walk through the valley of the shadow of death, I fear no evil, for You are with me; …" (v. 1, 4).

God had spared my life.

The dramatic series of events leading up to and following this fateful day started me on a journey that would forever change my life. I began to realize that life—and all its drama—was sometimes beyond my control. This was one of the first times I felt completely weak and helpless to deal with what was happening around me. But it wouldn't be the last.

HEAD-ON!

During the early morning hours of August 30, 1970, California Highway Patrol officers Gary Haley and Tom Long were performing routine duties patrolling the freeway between Ventura and Santa Paula, California. They followed several cars and prepared to stop one for speeding. Suddenly, the officers noticed cars ahead of them slowing and veering erratically, some swerving right, others left. Then they saw two headlights coming straight at them—a nightmare before their eyes—a wrong-way driver on the freeway.

A few minutes earlier, with a blood alcohol level of 0.18, the driver of a compact sedan had entered the freeway off-ramp driving head-on into the oncoming traffic. As she approached the police car, Officer Long turned on the electronic siren while Officer Haley aimed the spotlight at her to get her attention and yelled for her to pull over using the PA system. Anyone in their right mind could see the glaring spotlight and flashing red lights. Was she trying to commit suicide? She responded like a mummy in a tomb. Looking straight ahead, she kept driving into oncoming traffic. How long could this go on? Death— hers and perhaps innocent others—was inevitable if she weren't stopped immediately.

Traffic was too heavy for Officer Long to turn the patrol vehicle around. In desperation, he tried backing up along the shoulder of the freeway while steering clear of oncoming traffic—to no avail. They were quickly losing her. Then, finding an opening in the center divider, he shot across to the other side of the freeway and raced in an attempt to catch her. Once parallel, they continued flashing warnings at her for several miles. "We could see her … almost like sitting next to her," Haley said. "The red and white lights still did no good. I got on the outside PA system and started screaming at her to get over. He [Long] got on the electronic siren. She just continued looking straight ahead, driving up the freeway in the wrong direction. She never once turned to look." When the futility of their chase became obvious, Haley and Long attempted to warn oncoming traffic.

Despite their efforts, two approaching vehicles could not see the warning lights ahead.

At 1:40 a.m., I was driving one of those oncoming cars, returning from a youth trip to a Dodgers' baseball game. My passengers included my wife, Joanne, and four teenagers—Jerry Reich, Dennis Sprik, Larry Thiesen, and John Sigala. For several miles, an off-duty sheriff's deputy named Dan Bowlin drove sidebyside in the lane next to me. Through the window, I could see the badge on his uniform, so I kept a close eye on my speedometer. Ahead was a gentle, rolling hill—a familiar, welcoming site indicating home was just a few miles farther.

Suddenly, without warning, over the top of the hill, I saw two headlights coming straight at me. The glare was blinding. Officer Bowlin, traveling in the right lane, swerved to safety. Panicked, I swerved right but too late. The small compact car crashed into the left front of the car I was driving. The screaming, screeching sound of metal clashing and bending pierced the night as the two vehicles collided at a combined speed of a 130 miles per hour. The compact sedan was crushed like a cardboard box, killing the driver instantly.

"My God! They hit headon!" Haley yelled. Officer Long raced through the center divider with the patrol vehicle. Haley and Long jumped out of the car and ran toward us. Joanne crawled out of the car with blood streaming down her face and staggered toward the officers screaming, "Help us! Oh, my God, help us!" Two of the teenagers had managed to escape the car. The other two were in the back, one on the car seat, the other on the floor. Unconscious, I was trapped behind the mangled steering wheel.

Officer Haley crawled into the backseat of the car, pulling one teenager to safety as flames leaped from the engine compartment. Officer Long grabbed the fire extinguisher, shooting it at the flames to no avail. Haley then carried the other teenager to safety as the flames continued to spread. Five had been rescued; one was left in the car.

With the engine compartment in flames, the car obviously could explode at any moment. I was not only trapped behind the steering wheel, but the driver's side door was crushed. The officer yelled, "We've got to get him out of there." Realizing I was still in the car, Joanne crawled in the passenger side desperately working to pull me free from the burning vehicle. She couldn't pull me free. The strength of the crushed door certainly exceeded human strength. Special equipment would be required to open it. There was no time for a jaws-of-life rescue.

A pool of gasoline had spilled under and around the car. Aware they were walking in gasoline and risking their lives as the flames continued to spread, Dennis Sprik, one of the rescued teenagers, and Officers Haley and Bowlin approached the car. They put their full strength into opening the driver's side door that wouldn't budge. Dennis said the leaping flames from the engine compartment stopped short of the windshield, almost as if there were an invisible wall holding the flames back. Then a trail of gasoline from the car caught fire. The car would explode in seconds. In one final attempt, they pulled on the door, and it opened. As the smoke and heat grew in intensity, they grabbed me: "I couldn't extract Beckwith," Haley recalled. "If we didn't get him out, he was going to go. He was screaming. I knew I was hurting him, but I'd rather have him hurt than dead. The car was burning, and I was trying to get him out as best I could." With a final jerk, they pulled me free from the mangled dash and crumpled steering wheel pinning me inside the car. Just seconds later, as they laid me on the pavement, the car exploded in an inferno of flames. When I regained consciousness, I was lying in the middle of the freeway—shattered glass piercing my back while flames and flashing lights pierced the darkness. In the midst of this, I saw Joanne, looking like an angel, quoting the twenty-third Psalm.

My gratitude overflows to those who risked their lives to rescue me from the burning car. Officers Tom Long, Gary Haley, and Dan Bowlin each received the "Certificate of Accommodation for Meritorious Achievement" in recognition of their courage and bravery risking their lives in the line of duty. My life-long friend, Dennis Sprik, also risked his life in the rescue.[2]

As Joanne held me close during the ambulance ride to the hospital, I drifted in and out of consciousness. From adjoining beds in the emergency room, we discovered the physical injuries we each had suffered. I was writhing in pain with lacerations to my legs and chest, several broken teeth, and a broken wrist. I also had deep puncture wounds to both sides of my neck. Amazingly, the neck wounds hadn't lacerated the jugular veins. Joanne suffered a deep cut through her left cheek that went to the bone only a fraction of an inch from her eye. The surgery required three layers of stitches, but her eyesight was spared.

Once released from the hospital, we came face to face with our challenges—we were unemployed, with about two hundred dollars in savings, private school tuition to pay, medical bills in the thousands, no car, and a baby to feed and care for. We were grateful our two-month-old daughter, Julie, was with a babysitter the night of the accident.

Over the next few months, things went from bad to worse. Life was spinning wildly, and we were struggling to hang on. Physically, we were banged up and continued to be in pain. Emotionally, we were drained and discouraged. Financially, we were sinking, and our parents were in no position to assist us

---

2. Dennis Sprik speaks in churches, schools, and camps presenting the "Hands of the Potter" program. While speaking, Dennis shapes jars of clay to illustrate Jeremiah 18:6. Dave and Dennis have teamed together combining Dave's story with the "Hands of the Potter" program (www.handsofthepotter.net).

with medical expenses and college costs. Spiritually, we were at the end of our "hope rope." Little did we know this was exactly where God wanted us. He had lessons to teach us in our weakness.

DAY ONE—CHAPTER ONE:

TIME OUT

Power Thoughts for Your Time Alone With God

We were at the end of our "hope rope." Little did we know this was exactly where God wanted us. He had lessons to teach us in our weakness.

◊ Read Psalm 23, the chapter Joanne quoted after Dave's rescue from the burning car. Could you quote it to someone going through "the valley of the shadow of death" (v. 4)? As it has only six verses, this is a great chapter to commit to memory.

◊ Think of a time when you were at the end of your "hope rope." What was God teaching you?

◊ How does this Psalm speak to you regarding your past, present, and future?

◊ As you go back through Psalm 23, personalize it and pray your thoughts back to God. *My Lord, you are my shepherd. How awesome that you watch over me. You are aware of my every want, and you supply my every need.*

◊ Go to the back of your book for this week's meditation verses titled "God's Power Pack." Carry it with you or put it someplace where you can direct your thoughts to it throughout the day and memorize it.

FROM THE FRYING PAN INTO THE FIRE

The catastrophic car accident was just the beginning. In the months that followed, I found myself questioning God again and again: "Why is this happening?" An inexplicable series of setbacks invaded our lives. Our insurance company notified us our auto insurance rates would go up because I now had an accident on my record. "What? This isn't fair!" I protested to the insurance agent to no avail.

Since we were without a vehicle, Joanne's parents lent us a car. Less than a week later, in a rush to get to an appointment, I couldn't find the car. After searching the parking area and talking to the apartment manager to make sure the car had not been towed, I realized it had been stolen. Sinking in despair, I stood looking at the empty spot where I'd parked the car, asking God, "With car number-one burned and totaled and car number-two stolen, what are we supposed to do? Walk?" We filed a police report, but the car was never recovered. Joanne's dad didn't have the vehicle insured for theft, so we owed Joanne's parents for the stolen car, and we were still without an automobile.

As medical bills arrived stamped "Due and Payable Now," all I could do was stare in utter disbelief. The depression was overwhelming as the bills, mounting to thousands of dollars, buried us in debt. Meanwhile, I needed major dental reconstruction due to the broken teeth. Confused and disheartened, my attitude turned sour.

A week after the car was stolen, the stereo in our apartment caught fire, blackening the stair railing and walls. The fire and smoke also reignited the memories and fears of the accident.

A few weeks later, my billfold was stolen. Someone enjoyed a spending spree using our credit cards. Angry and resentful, I became obsessed with trying to track down and confront this person.

Joanne's dad lent us the money to buy a used car to get by, but we still had no money and no job. A few months prior to the accident, I had graduated from Biola with my Bachelor of Science degree in Business Administration. During my college years, I had received affirmation as a student leader and assumed the business world was excitedly awaiting my arrival. I was in for a big disappointment. I began applying for positions with various businesses, thinking some company would certainly want me as a junior executive. The chairman of the Biola Business Department, Bob Livingston, assured me a position would open up soon. For two months, I pursued every lead. To my dismay, I couldn't even get an interview. Finally, Bob Livingston called to say he had a job opening.

"What company?" I asked.

"Dart Transportation in Los Angeles."

"All right, finally, an interview," I replied. "What's the position and salary?"

"This may not be your dream position," Bob said, "but they have an opening for loading trucks on the evening shift, paying a little over minimum wage. You'll be working on the dock, loading Sears' freight for Dart Transportation."

What? A college degree so I could load trucks at night? My disappointment was obvious on the phone, but I needed a job. I went for the interview and got hired. During the year that followed, I worked the loading dock from 3:30 p.m. until all the freight was loaded—usually midnight, but sometimes two or three a.m. Biola classes for Joanne and Talbot Seminary classes for me started at 7:30 a.m. and dismissed at noon. Our infant daughter, Julie, stayed with a wonderful friend during the morning. When classes dismissed, we picked Julie up and shared a brief lunch together before studying and heading back to work.

I'd always been able to pull things through by relying on my strengths. But at this point, my strengths were no match for the avalanche of life problems. I began to face the fact that I was not only weak but had a lot of weaknesses. I became fearful, discouraged, and resentful. Joanne, struggling with vivid memories of the head-on crash and exploding car, experienced fear, which she shares in this next section.

SPINNING OUT OF CONTROL

[Joanne speaking] The Cinderella story I'd envisioned for my life became a nightmare. Over and over, my mind replayed the sounds of crushing metal and blaring sirens. It brought to mind the many attempts to pull Dave from the car, followed by the explosion, and finally wondering if Dave would die as he lay there on the pavement. My sleep was interrupted by fearful thoughts and dreams. I had difficulty feeling safe in a car and even felt vulnerable in our home, repeatedly checking the closets for intruders. Whenever I caught the smell of smoke, it set off an adrenaline surge, and my mind froze. When our home stereo caught fire and smoke poured out the back, I was paralyzed with panic. Something had happened to me; life seemed wildly out of control.

The refining process of purifying my faith was set in motion in my life. I had to grow stronger, to learn more fully who God was and is and why I can trust him. Without this confidence, I had no real security.

DAY TWO—CHAPTER ONE

TIME OUT
Power Thoughts for Your Time Alone With God

When troubles come your way, consider it an opportunity for great joy.
—James 1:2 NLT

◊ What circumstances in your life are stretching your faith? Are they perplexing? Discouraging? Do you feel beaten?

◊ Read James 1:2-12.

◊ Have you ever thought of trials and temptations as friends? Check out this paraphrase of James 1:2-5:

> When all kinds of trials and temptations crowd into your lives my brothers, don't resent them as intruders, but welcome them as friends! Realize that they come to test your faith and to produce in you the quality of endurance. But let the process go on until that endurance is fully developed, and you will find you have become men of mature character with the right sort of independence. And if, in the process, any of you does not know how to meet any particular problem he has only to ask God—who gives generously to all men without making them feel foolish or guilty—and he may be quite sure that the necessary wisdom will be given him. (PHILLIPS NT)

As you pray …

1. Ask God to give you a different attitude about your trials—to even welcome them.
2. Ask God to use your trials to shape and mature you.
3. Ask God for wisdom and patience to respond to each challenge.

REFINING GOLD

Faith grows in the struggles and pressures of life as God teaches us to depend on him. James McConkey said it this way: "Faith is dependence upon God. And this God-dependence only begins when self-dependence ends. And self-dependence only comes to its end, with some of us, when sorrow, suffering, affliction, broken plans and hopes bring us to that place of self-helplessness and defeat."[3]

Life is painful and perplexing—disappointments, sorrows, broken dreams and aspirations, conflicts, misunderstandings. When life is heartbreaking and agonizing, you may wonder, *Why didn't God make life a little smoother? I hope there's a reason for this pain because it doesn't make much sense.* I assure you, there *is* a purpose, a bigger plan behind the struggle.

When your dreams come tumbling down, when someone stabs you in the back, when your health deteriorates, when you try and fail, when you're abandoned and lonely, Christ invites you to himself. He has experienced pain far beyond any suffering you can comprehend, and his love for you is greater than the love of any of your friends or family. When you are wounded and hurting, read Isaiah 53—the predictions of the suffering and death of Christ—feeling the wounds he felt and applying his healing to your life: "He was pierced for our rebellion, crushed for our sins. He was beaten so we could be whole. He was whipped so we could be healed" (Isa. 53:5 NLT).

Without brokenness, it's easy to drift along—self-sufficient, seemingly strong, judgmental and self-righteous, demanding of others and often blaming them, expecting to be served rather than serving, unmoved by the pain of others, and an all-around nuisance to live with. With crushing and breaking, you become keenly aware of your weaknesses, valuing others over yourself,

---

3. Miles J. Stanford, *Principles of Spiritual Growth* (Lincoln, NB: Back to the Bible Publication, 1979), 9.

and yielding rights. You respond to others with graciousness, humbled by how much you need to learn. You become willing to forgive others with the awareness of your need for forgiveness, developing compassion for others when they hurt. Your faith deepens and matures. This is the process the first-century believers were going through when Peter encouraged them with these words: "In this you greatly rejoice, even though now for a little while, if necessary, you have been distressed by various trials, so that the proof of your faith, *being* more precious than gold which is perishable, even though tested by fire, may be found to result in praise and glory and honor at the revelation of Jesus Christ" (1 Pet. 1:6-7).

The process of refining gold is a vivid illustration of God's refining process. A hunk of gold ore doesn't look like much before being refined. First in the refining process, machines called crushers reduce large chunks of ore to the size of road gravel. Crushing is the first prerequisite. In the life of a believer, God works to crush hardness and defiance. Next, the gold ore is subjected to the smelting process. Gold melts at 1948° F (1064° C). This extreme heat is necessary to remove the impurities. Smelting involves melting the gold in a furnace with a chemical mixture called flux, which combines with the impurities and floats on top of the gold. The dross can then be skimmed or poured off. Repeated heating brings the impurities to the surface, and the skimming continues until all the impurities are removed. *In the final test of pure gold, the goldsmith can see his reflection in the gold.*

When the heat is on in your life, impurities will surface—arrogance, a sour attitude, irritability, an independent streak, jealousy, overeating, substance abuse, or anger. The natural tendency is to be horrified with what comes to the surface. Disappointment in self comes from believing in self. Your failure didn't catch God off-guard. Don't beat yourself up with your failure. Be patient with yourself—God is at work. "One of God's most effective means in the process is failure. So many believers are simply frantic over the fact of failure in their lives, and they will go to all lengths in trying to hide it, ignore it, or rationalize about it."[4] Acknowledge your failure and ask God to skim it from your life. "Failure where self is concerned in our Christian life and service is allowed and often engineered by God in order to turn us completely from ourselves to his source for our life—Christ Jesus, who never fails."[5]

Heat, pressure, failure, doubts, skimming off the impurities, more heat, trials, temptations, more removing of impurities— the goldsmith knows what he's doing. *The final test is when the goldsmith, Jesus Christ, sees his perfect reflection in you. Pure gold!*

4. Stanford, *Principles of Spiritual Growth*, 24.
5. Stanford, 24.

DAY THREE—CHAPTER ONE

TIME OUT
Power Thoughts for Your Time Alone With God

Disappointment in self comes from believing in self.

◊ Read and reflect on 1 Peter 1:3–9.

◊ When have you been disappointed in yourself?

◊ What tends to come to the surface (lashing out, bad attitude, overeating, driving like a maniac, etc.) when the heat is on in your life?

◊ Ask God to skim the impurities from your life.

POWER IN WEAKNESS

When you're discouraged, beat up, or resentful, God's awesome power is available for you in your weakness. This is "strength in weakness"—a new way of living, a God-empowering attitude that changes how you approach life. When God's power is fused with your weakness, the results are astounding. These three weakness-to-strength principles build sequentially— the first laying the foundation for the second, and the second a prerequisite for the third. This is your edge—your unique advantage to experience a God-empowered life.

First, be God-secure.

A core belief in God—that he is in control, that he loves you and wants the best for you—provides the foundation for being God-secure. In him, you are loved, and you begin to live like someone who is loved. You carry yourself differently. You're not as rattled when others are falling apart. The approval of others becomes less important. You're moving forward and doing great ... and then it happens. You slip and fall and feel deeply disappointed. As you ask for forgiveness and sense him picking you up, you realize he wasn't shocked or surprised by your stumble. In fact, he knew it was coming. It was part of his plan to teach and shape you. You further realize Jesus loves you on your beautiful days as well as your bummer days. You're not on probation. His love never fluctuates; it's eternal. As this love becomes deeply internalized in your psyche and incorporated into the way you live, your faith grows stronger, more secure.

Like the slow lifting of a thick fog, some of the struggles and disappointments from the past start to make sense. You begin to have a clearer picture of what happened and why, and more importantly, how God was using it to shape you. You learn to rest secure in his love.

Sometimes you'll see a surprising benefit from what seemed to be a tragedy. After the accident, Joanne's sense of smell became amazingly sharp, and her adrenalin surged when she smelled smoke. One Sunday morning, she woke up smelling smoke, which I didn't notice. She called the fire department, and they discovered a smoldering outlet in the wall. The fire department said that without her keen sense of smell, our home would have burned to the ground while we were at church.

What helped Joanne grow in being God-secure? Meditating and claiming the truths in the following verses set her free from her fearful thoughts and restless sleep.

> "Do not tremble; do not be afraid. Did I not proclaim my purposes for you long ago? You are my witnesses—is there any other God? No! There is no other Rock—not one!" (Isa. 44:8 NLT)

> The LORD is my rock, my fortress, and my savior; my God is my rock, in whom I find protection. He is my shield, the power that saves me, and my place of safety. (Ps. 18:2 NLT)

> "I am the LORD, the God of all the peoples of the world. Is anything too hard for me?" (Jer. 32:27 NLT)

> "For I know the plans that I have for you," declares the LORD, "plans for welfare and not for calamity to give you a future and a hope." (Jer. 29:11)

Meditate on these verses for a week and see how they change your outlook. You'll increase your faith in who God is, in his power, and in the knowledge that you can trust him. Knowledge of your awesome God and how secure you are in him will flood your thoughts.

If all of this is new to you, you may ask, "How do I begin this relationship with God?" It's as simple as the ABC's. There are three simple steps to being "eternally loved and secure." Go to the back of this book and look for the page titled "Three Simple Steps to New Life" (Appendix A). Pray the prayer at the end as you begin your new relationship with God. This is the most important decision you will ever make in your life. Secure in your new relationship, your faith can grow. The more you learn about God's character, the more God-secure you become when life hits you head-on.

DAY FOUR—CHAPTER ONE

TIME OUT

Power Thoughts for Your Time Alone With God

A core belief in God—that he is in control, that he loves you and wants the best for you—provides a foundation for being God-secure.

◊ Read Psalm 18:1–6.

◊ Make some notes of when you were highly stressed or possibly felt your life was threatened.

◊ On a scale of 1–5 (5 being high), how secure do you feel in the following areas:

    ___ My family
    ___ My job
    ___ My investments
    ___ My friends
    ___ My health
    ___ My traveling (auto, airplane, etc.)
    ___ My retirement
    ___ My reputation
    ___ My income and expenses
    ___ The economy
    ___ World events

_____ My eternal destiny

◊ Which issues from the above list are most difficult for you?

◊ Look back and reflect on the verses mentioned earlier in this section (Is. 44:8, Ps. 18:2, Jer. 32:27 and 29:11) and apply them to your greatest areas of fear. Focus on these verses as you pray.

SECOND, BE GOD-SURRENDERED.

Surrender is not our usual mode of operation. Instead, when we feel insecure, we lash out, grow stubborn, sulk, or get angry—anything but surrender. This is why being God-secure precedes being God-surrendered. The stronger your core belief that God is completely reliable, the easier it will be for you to surrender your life and future to him.

In my insecurities, I was a fighter, always struggling and striving. The idea of being weak was unthinkable. When I read "power is perfected in weakness" and "when I am weak, then I am strong" (2 Cor. 12:9, 10), I honestly didn't have a clue what this meant. How could weakness be the key to strength? Everything I knew argued otherwise. I believed that to succeed, I had to be strong. To conquer, I had to take control. To win, I couldn't appear weak. The success-driven model I aspired to applauded strength, charisma, self-sufficiency, and hard work. Weakness was for wimps and losers.

For many years, even with the awareness of my weaknesses, I tried to succeed in my own strength. I was always striving, trying harder, resolving to do better—still thinking I was the source of strength. When I failed, I'd berate myself rather than accept the life-changing truth: *I was trying to do it myself—while God was trying to bring me to the end of myself.*

We like to feel we can handle what comes our way. Instead, God allows huge challenges that leave us weak-kneed and wobbly—challenges like getting out of debt, completing a degree while caring for four children and holding a full-time job, dealing with chronic pain, overcoming an addiction, raising an autistic child, grieving the loss of a loved one. Does the challenge you face leave you feeling weak in the lining of your soul? Good. To the weary, God gives strength, and he increases the power of the weak (Isa. 40:29).

Being God-secure doesn't happen all at once and learning to be God-surrendered is a process. Through the years, you'll likely repeat the steps many times—a new experience of trusting and yielding followed by renewed strength. Philippians 3:10 becomes a lived-out process: 1) knowing Christ more deeply in the fellowship of his suffering (becoming God-secure); 2) experiencing conformity to his death (being God-surrendered); and 3) knowing the power of his resurrection (being God-strengthened). Surrender is the prelude to strength; it is God's power when you're exhausted; it is God taking over when you feel you've miserably failed. Your moment of weakness is the beginning of his strength.

THIRD, BE GOD-STRENGTHENED.

Your personal resources are limited. Even the young grow tired and weary. Those in their prime will stumble and fall. "Those who wait upon GOD get fresh strength. They spread their wings and soar like eagles, they run and don't get tired, they walk and don't lag behind" (Isa. 40:31 MSG). God has promised his power will be perfected in your weakness.

How would you complete this sentence? I can do everything through _____. Some would say, "My education … my exceptional talents … my problem-solving abilities … my perseverance … my ability to work with people." Paul said, "I can do everything through Christ, who gives me strength" (Phil. 4:13 NLT). Don't overlook the three words "everything through

Christ." He will supply strength for whatever is in his plan for your life.

So why not take the first step of surrender and strike the match? Surrender lights the fire of God's power.

And here's your "power pack" of promises, fuel that keeps the fire going.

> I can do all things through him
> who strengthens me.
> Greater is he who is in me than
> he who is in the world.
> I am more than a conqueror
> through him who loves me.
> Absolutely nothing is impossible with God!
> (Phil. 4:13, 1 John 4:4, Rom. 8:37, and Luke 1:37 first
> person paraphrase)

Claim them, repeat them, memorize them, prove them, and when life hits you head-on, thrust your arms in the air and whisper a shout:

> GOD, YOU PROMISED—I AM MORE THAN A
> CONQUEROR ... I CAN DO ALL THINGS THROUGH
> YOU ... NOTHING IS IMPOSSIBLE IN YOUR
> STRENGTH ... YOU ARE GREATER THAN ANYTHING
> LIFE THROWS AT ME!

This is *your winning edge* to turn weakness into victory.

DAY FIVE—CHAPTER ONE

TIME OUT

Power Thoughts for Your Time Alone With God

Strike the match. Surrender lights the fire of God's power.

◊ Read Romans 8:28–39. Below is a first person paraphrase of verses 31-39.

If God is for me, who can be against me? He who did not spare his own Son, but gave him up for me—how will he not also, along with him, graciously give me all things?

Who will bring any charge against me whom God has chosen? It is God who justifies. Who is he that condemns? Christ Jesus, who died—more than that, who was raised to life—is at the right hand of God and is also interceding for me.

Who shall separate me from the love of Christ? Shall trouble or hardship or persecution or famine or nakedness or danger or sword? As it is written: "For your sake we face death all day long; we are considered as sheep to be slaughtered." No, in all these things I am more than a conqueror through him who loved me.

For I am convinced that neither death nor life, neither angels nor demons, neither the present nor the future, nor any powers, neither height nor depth, nor anything else in all creation, will be able to separate me from the love of God that is in Christ Jesus my Lord. (Rom. 8:31-39, paraphrased in the first person)

◊ What phrases in this passage fill you with an overwhelming sense of being secure?

◊ Pray a prayer of surrender. Tell God you voluntarily relinquish your will to his power and authority. Make note of specific areas you are choosing to release.

TIME TOGETHER

SESSION ONE

HEAD-ON WITH LIFE

If you've tried really hard to succeed but found yourself floundering and failing, you're going to love what you discover in this session. We're going to look at how to face the tough stuff in life and what happens when God fuses his power with our weakness. Three weakness-to-strength principles will be applied: 1) be God-secure, 2) be God-surrendered, and 3) be God-strengthened. This is your winning edge—your unique advantage to experiencing a God-empowered life. Let's get started in this exciting session.

A GUIDE FOR SMALL GROUPS

If you're leading the group, read the Guide for Small Groups in Appendix B. Included in that guide are tools you will find very helpful for a successful group experience:

1) Tips for Leading a Small Group

2) Tips for Hosting a Small Group

3) Small Group Guidelines (discuss this as a group in your first session)

4) Ask and You Shall Receive (write down prayer requests and answers to prayer)

5) God's VIPs (your group roster, with contact information)

CONNECT

◊ Start with an "autograph-signing party." VIPs sign autographs and every person in the group is one of God's "very important people." Hand your book around the circle and have each person sign it and include contact information (email address and phone number). Ask them to print their information since the autographs of most VIPs are impossible to read. Use the worksheet titled "God's VIPs," included in the small-group guide (Appendix B).

◊ As an alternative, you can have everyone put their name and contact information on a sheet of paper. After the session, have someone word process this and email it to everyone.

◊ As a group, read and discuss aloud the "Small Group Guidelines" included in the small-group guide (Appendix B).

GROW

◊ The 23rd Psalm is one of the most loved sections in the Bible. Read Psalm 23 in the two translations below. Have one or more group members read this aloud.

The LORD is my shepherd, I shall not want. He makes me lie down in green pastures; He leads me beside quiet waters. He restores my soul; He guides me in the paths of righteousness For His name's sake.Even though I walk through the valley of the shadow of death, I fear no evil, for You are with me; Your rod and Your staff, they comfort me. You prepare a table before me in the presence of my enemies; You have anointed my head with oil; My cup overflows. Surely goodness and lovingkindness will follow me all the days of my life, And I will dwell in the house of the LORD forever. (Ps. 23:1-6)

The LORD is my shepherd; I have all that I need. He lets me rest in green meadows; he leads me beside peaceful streams. He renews my strength. He guides me along right paths, bringing honor to his name. Even when I walk through the darkest valley, I will not be afraid, for you are close beside me. Your rod and your staff protect and comfort me. You prepare a feast for me in the presence of my enemies. You honor me by anointing my head with oil. My cup overflows with blessings. Surely your goodness and unfailing love will pursue me all the days of my life, and I will live in the house of the LORD forever. (Ps. 23:1-6 NLT)

◊ Share a time when this psalm was especially meaningful to you.

◊ In what ways are human beings like sheep?

◊ What in this psalm helps you be God-secure? Write the group answers on a poster board, if one is available.

◊ What have you discovered in this psalm that helps you want to be God-surrendered?

◊ In what ways do you feel "God-strengthened," knowing what you've discovered in this chapter?

APPLY

◊ Have fun with the group, discussing these "think-it-through" statements.

1. If you love God, walk with Him, and take care of yourself in appropriate ways, it is impossible for you to die one day short of the number of days God intended for you to live.   True – False – Uncertain

2. If you eat mostly junk foods, drive fast and recklessly, abuse alcohol or drugs, it is impossible for you to die one day short of the number of days God intended for you to live.   True – False – Uncertain

◊ What situations have made it particularly difficult for you to trust God?

◊ What has led you to a point of surrender (if you have come to this point)? If not, what holds you back?

PRAY

◊ Begin with some quiet moments of heart examination. Pray silently, "Lord, I surrender those areas in my life where I have tried and failed."

◊ One at a time read the four verses below from "God's Power Pack" aloud. After each verse, pray and claim the verse for your life.

God's Power Pack
I can do all things through
him who strengthens me.
Greater is he who is in
me than he who is in the
world.
I am more than a
conqueror through him
who loves me.
Absolutely nothing is
impossible with God!
—Phil. 4:13; 1 John 4:4;
Rom. 8:37; Luke 1:37
(paraphrase)

◊ Optional: if someone plays an instrument, ask that person to lead in a song of praise. Or select a song on a Christian CD and play it as the group sings along. Make certain the song isn't too difficult for group singing.

SHARE

◊ Do you know of someone who's going through a tough time? Reach out to him or her—a caring phone call, an encouraging text or email, or get together for coffee or a meal.

◊ Ask God to use you to show kindness to someone this week. Look for an opportunity to start a conversation. When the moment is right, here are some starter questions:

1. Have you ever had a moment when you thought you were a goner? Did someone swerve into your lane? Were you in an earthquake, tornado, or hurricane? Did you experience a frightening airline flight?

2. What went through your mind? How did this impact you?

◊ Use your own wording. It may or may not happen but be prepared to respond if someone turns the question back to you. You may have an opportunity to explain how God has protected your life and what your relationship with Christ means.

EXTRAS

◊ For insight on Psalm 23, check out the book by Phillip Keller, *A Shepherd Looks at Psalm 23* (Grand Rapids, Michigan: Zondervan Publishing House, 1970). Have someone bring a brief summary of how each phrase in Psalm 23 relates to a shepherd with his sheep.

◊ This is an optional discussion story if time permits. Have you ever awakened in the middle of the night with a heavy burden to pray for someone? Go to prayer immediately. You never know what may be taking place in their life. Pray for that person until God allows you to go back to sleep. Vivian Bolt, a longtime member of Woodbridge Community Church where I served as pastor, shared this story with me. Her son, Pastor Ron Bolt, confirmed the details of the story.

The Lord awakened me at 5:00 a.m. California time. I sensed that the International Interns Inc. Rezina Missions Team ministering in Moldova, a country in southeastern Europe bordered by Romania on the west and by Ukraine on the other three sides, was in serious danger. My son, Pastor Ron Bolt, was leading the short-term missions team. Not knowing anything specific, I prayed earnestly for two hours without knowing that in Moldova it was precisely 3:00 p.m. to 5:00 p.m. After praying, I felt release and peace from the Lord that everything was okay. Later I found out that at the time I was awakened, the Rezina ministry team was approaching the village of Tarosova for a 3:00 p.m. service. An angry confrontation by villagers took place that threatened an outbreak of violence. It was a time of great danger. Someone reached the mayor by cell phone, and even though he was at a major soccer event in another community, he rushed to [the group's] aid. Only the Lord knows what actual violence might have taken place had he not arrived at this very troubling scene and finally convinced the angry mob that the group had the legal right to hold the meeting. The confrontation finally settled down at 5:00 p.m. and all parties parted peacefully. The team returned the following year to Tarosova without any resistance whatsoever, and we learned authorities had communicated clearly to this village that such an incident must never be repeated.

CHAPTER TWO

DISCOVERING POWER IN WEAKNESS

*A great weakness is a pretense of strength; a great strength is
a humble acknowledgment of weakness.*

God could easily have designed us so every year we grow stronger, better-looking, sexier, and healthier. It would have been easy for the Creator to pre-program us with steadily improving eyesight, hearing, and sense of smell while our teeth became whiter and our hair thicker. The young would aspire to get old. The old would get some respect. "Don't mess with him. He's a 125-year-old hunk, and he'll clean your clock." Just imagine having your photo taken every year to place it next to last year's photo as you congratulate yourself, *Wow, I'm getting better-looking every day.*

Obviously, God designed the program to operate in reverse. Every year our physical bodies develop new aches, and something that worked fine last year now sputters. Yes, we're weak and getting weaker. Why? God is clearly up to something but before getting into the why, let's examine the four types of weaknesses: personal limitations, personal woundedness, personal sin bent, and personal weakness from the misuse of strengths.

FOUR TYPES OF WEAKNESSES

To be successful, many think they need to impress others with their strengths and make certain no one discovers their flat side. But as strange as it sounds, admitting we're weak, frail human beings is the first step toward becoming strong. *A great weakness is a pretense of strength; a great strength is a humble acknowledgment of weakness. The fear of appearing weak is a weakness.* "Power in weakness" is a transforming mindset, an exciting new way of living, your winning edge in a scary world.

As you identify your weaknesses in this section, you are taking the first steps to launch God's power in a new way in your life. Let's look at the four types of weaknesses.

TYPE ONE: PERSONAL LIMITATIONS

The majority of our weaknesses stem from the fact we're human. As a result, we have limitations in our bodies, minds, and personalities. Our mortal bodies are inherently "decaying," which means most of us face some physical issue (or issues). Some of these may be minimal and sometimes humorous while others are humiliating and difficult.

For years I lived in denial of one of my physical weaknesses, one that brought great irritation to anyone within earshot. I was a "hardcore snorer," and I tried to deny it. When confronted, I quickly shot back, "What? Me snore? I didn't hear anything. I was there the whole night." This usually stirred a friendly argument.

Then my brother attacked my denial head-on. He recorded me one Sunday afternoon while I was flaked out on the couch. *Zzzzzz-ZZzzZz-hnggggh-Ppbhww-zZZzzzZZ.* To make matters worse, he recorded it at the end of one of our favorite musicals, *Fiddler on the Roof,* and he cranked the volume up, so it rattled the speakers. It was horrible. This was in the days of the old reel-to-reel tapes, and I couldn't figure out how to erase it. So every time we played *Fiddler on the Roof*, it concluded with this hideous version of "the old man is snoring."

Denial no longer worked so I changed my tactic. I declared that people who snore in their sleep are *happy*. "Snoring," I argued, "is the serene vibrations of a truly contented person, somewhat like the sound of ocean waves going out and coming in." No one agreed with me, but when I came downstairs in the morning and heard, "Dad, you were really happy last night," everyone laughed—and everyone knew what that meant. Eventually, I received a diagnosis of sleep apnea, and now I use a breathing mask, which eliminates snoring.

Many people live with more serious issues such as visual or hearing impairments, loss of an arm or leg, life-threatening diseases, or chronic physical pain. Daily life can be challenging and disheartening. Some impairments, such as fatigue, lupus, dyslexia, dizziness, dysfunctional internal organs, emotional illnesses, and insomnia, are not readily visible to others. The invisibility of the limitation often leads to misunderstanding and adds an extra level of stress. Other limitations may be less impairing but still embarrassing like forgetfulness, deficiencies in math, science, spelling, or grammar, being non-athletic, being directionally challenged, and so on.

When Our Weakness Torments Us

Paul's physical weakness—his thorn in the flesh—was a source of irritation, anguish, and torment. "… to keep me from exalting myself, there was given me a thorn in the flesh, a messenger of Satan to torment me—to keep me from exalting myself! Concerning this I implored the Lord three times that it might leave me" (2 Cor. 12:7-8).

Many have speculated about what Paul's thorn in the flesh was—poor eyesight, malaria, or migraine headaches. John

MacArthur raises the possibility that the thorn in the flesh was Paul's adversaries who fiercely opposed his work. The Greek word for "thorn" means a "sharp stake," and one possibility is malaria-induced headaches that may have felt like stakes being driven into his head. Others suggest Paul had poor eyesight or an eye infection since he says in his letter to the Galatians, "See with what large letters I am writing to you with my own hand" (Gal. 6:11). However, when we consider all the possibilities, we still can't be sure.

The word used for "torment" is a Greek word that means to "beat or strike with the fist." Figuratively, Satan used Paul's thorn in the flesh to beat him up. Paul pleaded in prayer three times for his thorn in the flesh to be removed, but God's answer, using the once-for-all verb tense, was clear: "My grace is sufficient for you, for power is perfected in weakness" (2 Cor. 12:9). Until Paul accepted this limitation, Satan used it to discourage and defeat him. Once he was at peace with it, God uniquely displayed his power. The weakness became God's "power point"—a visual display of his power on the screen of Paul's life.

Do you have a personal limitation—an agonizing deficiency, chronic pain, or disease—that Satan uses to "beat you up"? Do you feel tormented by it? You've likely prayed about it pleading for God to remove it. God may or may not heal it. If the limitation continues, don't lose heart. God has a unique purpose that he wants to display through your life.

I've witnessed miraculous healings so I have no question God can supernaturally cure incurable diseases. God used Paul to heal others, but in this case, the healer wasn't healed. God used Paul's weakness in two ways: 1) as an antidote to pride; and 2) as an amplification of God's power in his life. In the book of 2 Corinthians, Paul gives an inside look into his personal journal. He includes his feelings of inadequacy, moments of despair, persecutions, and how he appropriated God's strength.

Personality Weaknesses

Different from physical limitations, personality weaknesses are those pesky character flaws each of us has whether we like to admit it or not. These shortcomings remind us that in our own strength, we are utterly weak and helpless. But in God's power, our weaknesses can become great strengths.

Most people who know me assume I'm a naturally organized neat-freak. Not so. This is a learned behavior. The home I grew up in was messy, a vast collection of "never-know-when-I-may-need-this" stuff. If a thief had broken into our house while we were out of town, he would have thought someone had already broken in and ransacked the place. The yard and the basement where I slept overflowed with discarded auto parts, bicycles, lawnmowers, refrigerator motors, and hundreds of other items. My dad could fix anything with a part off something he had collected. I slept in the junk-filled basement on an army cot—ignoring the sounds of dad working into the night with his power tools and the constant clatter of the rock tumbler. My dad also had fifty to sixty junk cars he kept in a cow pasture. Now and then, he'd get suspicious someone was stealing parts from his cars. To catch a thief, my brothers slept out there. They never caught anyone, but they considered it a high adventure. In addition, my dad visited dumps all over South Dakota to find and bring stuff home. Collecting junk and hoarding was in my DNA.

I was a sloppy, messy kid. In fifth grade, my desk must have looked like a natural disaster with stacks of papers sticking out of the desktop and piles of books and papers stashed underneath. The teacher stopped at my desk one afternoon and pointed out to the class what a mess my desk was. The embarrassment stayed with me and later inspired me to get serious about cleaning up my act.

As a teenager, I had a well-deserved reputation for being scatterbrained and forgetful. Time and time again, I'd forget an important event or school assignment. My friends tagged me "Daze" instead of "Dave." It was embarrassing. Finally, after forgetting to show for an important event and being publicly humiliated, I decided to do something about it. I purchased a calendar and notepad and began writing things down. This was the beginning of getting my life organized.

I don't function well if things get too scattered, nor do I handle multi-tasking well. I may have some natural organizational ability, but this tendency to be forgetful and scattered forces me to be organized and focused. I've leveraged my scatter-brained weakness into what most people consider a strength—being organized.

[Joanne speaking] I struggled with shyness and timidity throughout grade school and high school and spoke very softly. My senior yearbook acknowledged this by choosing the phrase, "A soft answer turns away wrath" (Prov. 15:1) to place under my picture—a nice way of saying I was very quiet.

My dad gave me the book *How to Win Friends and Influence People* by Dale Carnegie, which had a great impact on me. When I left for college at Biola, I decided with the Lord's help, I'd get out of my comfort zone and reach out to others. The opportunity came through my job in the campus cafeteria, where I recorded meal-ticket numbers. I resolved to say something kind or encouraging to each person who came through the meal line. This was a joy as I watched faces light up from my comments to them. It also landed me some dates—an unexpected perk. The experience of reaching out to encourage others changed a lot of things for me. I became comfortable putting the spotlight on others, and my confidence grew. It's how I met Dave (meal-ticket number 573), and it prepared me for my future role as a pastor's wife, leading ministries, and teaching.

DAY ONE—CHAPTER TWO

TIME OUT

Power Thoughts for Your Time Alone With God

Paul knew better than to pretend to be an all-sufficient tower of strength, a brilliant know-it-all. He often felt weak and inadequate.

◊ Read Matthew 5:3–10. To expand your thinking, the verses from the New American Standard Version are followed by a paraphrase in italics.

Blessed are the poor in spirit, for theirs is the kingdom of heaven. *You're blessed when you're at the end of your rope. With less of you there is more of God and his rule.* (MSG)

Blessed are those who mourn, for they shall be comforted. *You're blessed when you feel you've lost what is most dear to you. Only then can you be embraced by the One most dear to you.* (MSG)

Blessed are the gentle, for they shall inherit the earth. *God blesses those who are humble, for they will inherit the whole earth.* (NLT)

Blessed are those who hunger and thirst for righteousness, for they shall be satisfied. *You're blessed when you've worked up a good appetite for God. He's food and drink in the best meal you'll ever eat.* (MSG)

Blessed are the merciful, for they shall receive mercy. *God blesses those people who are merciful. They will be treated with mercy!* (CEV)

Blessed are the pure in heart, for they shall see God. *You're blessed when you get your inside world—your mind and heart—put right.* (MSG)

Blessed are the peacemakers, for they shall be called sons of God. *You're blessed when you can show people how to cooperate instead of compete or fight.* (MSG)

Blessed are those who have been persecuted for the sake of righteousness, for theirs is the kingdom of heaven. *God blesses those people who are treated badly for doing right. They belong to the kingdom of heaven.* (CEV)

◊ Look back over the eight beatitudes. What do you observe about how God will bless you even in weakness?

◊ Pray through the beatitudes asking God to build these character qualities in your life.

◊ Go to the back of your book for this week's meditation verse titled "Power Perfected in Weakness." Carry it with you or put it someplace where you can direct your thoughts to it throughout the day and memorize it.

TYPE TWO: PERSONAL WOUNDEDNESS

If you're alive and breathing, you have experienced hurts, disappointments, and personal woundedness. These are part of the package called life, and they play a role in shaping who you are. Your wounds may be related to your family and upbringing, social or economic circumstances, your personal past (including poor choices), unfair treatment, or injustice. If you're fired unjustly, you still have a blemish on your employment record. Those who have a felony on their record or have served time in prison have a tough road ahead. Generally, society does not offer grace for shortcomings. Thankfully, God does. He's there for the broken, the inadequate, and the downtrodden. He offers grace that turns weaknesses into strengths, limitations into possibilities, and liabilities into assets.

The apostle Paul experienced personal woundedness—physical beatings, imprisonments, shipwreck, false accusations, being deserted by co-workers, to name a few (2 Cor. 11:24-29; 2 Tim. 4:9-18). This could have pushed him over the edge to ruin and self-pity; instead, his woundedness became his cutting edge to experience God's strength in his weakness. Rather than letting personal woundedness take him down, Paul said, "Therefore I am well content with weaknesses, with insults, with distresses, with persecutions, with difficulties, for Christ's sake; for when I am weak, then I am strong" (2 Cor. 12:10).

[Dave speaking] My personal story of woundedness began with growing up in an angry home. My dad's anger communicated that I was unacceptable, and I learned to bury my feelings. He was a driven workaholic and demanded the same level of performance from me. To try to gain his approval, I became a driven workaholic and perfectionist. Sometimes without warning, my dad's wrath would flare, and he'd whip out his belt and start swinging it every which way. If I could escape, I ran and didn't come home until the early hours of the morning. If I couldn't get away, I hunkered down in a corner trying to protect myself. Since I was often mouthy and stubborn, I honestly felt I deserved the rage that sometimes accelerated into a beating.

I feared being around my dad not knowing when he would explode so I spent as little time at home as possible. Once when I was playing in the school band, he was upset that I was not working in his shop. He came in while the band was playing, grabbed me by my shirt, and pulled me physically out of the room and down three flights of stairs to the car. I was embarrassed in front of my friends and fuming with anger. Without someone to talk with, I internalized my anger and buried my feelings inside.

When I left home for California at age eighteen, I assumed I was leaving all that behind. My college years were a refreshing change, and I did quite well. After college and seminary, I entered the ministry. However, as the years went by, I came face to face with the unhealed issues in my life. My biggest problem was that "wherever I went, there I was."[6] I was the problem.

Some twenty years after entering the ministry, I met with a pastoral counselor. One afternoon, he asked me to tell him about my relationship with my father. I stiffened. I didn't want to talk about that subject. That was a long time ago. My father had passed away a decade earlier, and I didn't see any relevance in talking about it. But he urged me, "I think it's important for you to revisit that relationship. Take some time this week to write your memories of your relationship with your father."

Alone that week with a blank sheet of paper, I began to write my memories, and the tears flowed. I wrote page after page until I hit a buried pain, and then the tears started again. I discovered I wasn't bitter or angry with my father. More than anything else, I ached for a relationship we never had. I would have been thrilled to see him cheering in the stands even once when I played basketball, baseball, and football. When I played the lead roles

6. Jon Kabat-Zinn wrote a book titled *Wherever You Go, There You Are* (New York: Hyperion, 1994).

in school plays, I asked him to attend, but he was too busy. He was absent for my high school graduation. I had an aching hole in my life for my father's love. I needed his approval, but never felt I was good enough to receive it. His blessing was always just out of reach, and his anger resonated in my insecurities. I came to realize that the nearly non-existent relationship with my dad was also my fault since I'd rejected him, failing to accept him as a person. I longed to reverse this, to reach out and tell him I loved him and hear him say, "I love you."

When I shared my journaling with the pastoral counselor, I was surprised when he said, "You've suffered some major trauma and damage, and it's still affecting you as a husband, father, and pastor." He helped me understand I was still acting out the learned response of cowering in the corner like the eight-year-old boy of the past. When attacked, whether as a church leader or a husband and father, I responded like a little kid hunkering down in a corner or fleeing the scene. I internalized my feelings, beat myself up, escaped, and sometimes became depressed.

I was a grown man in my forties with little-boy insecurities. The pastoral counselor worked with me to deal with my issues. What I needed was to feel accepted and valued apart from performance. I knew the theology of God's love, but I hadn't allowed it to sink deep into my sense of worth. As I began my new journey, I allowed Jesus to embrace the total me—the good, the bad, and the ugly. Knowing God had forgiven and totally accepted me reached deep into my shattered sense of worth and value. Christ's complete love and acceptance began to change my thoughts and responses when criticized or attacked.

Strength Potential in Weaknesses

Weaknesses often have a hidden strength and discovering the potential of a weakness can be life-transforming. Personal limitations, inadequacies, and woundedness can develop into strengths by accepting them and applying God's grace to them. While the following list is neither exhaustive nor absolute, it gives some exciting possibilities of what God can do.

Weakness	Potential Strength
Abused	Advocate for the hurting
Anxious	Prayerful
Brokenhearted	Merciful
Daydreaming	Imaginative, creative
Depressed	Hungry for God
Difficulty sleeping	Devoted to prayer
Disadvantaged	Determined
Disabled	Compassionate
Disillusioned	Focused on the eternal
Easily offended	Sensitive to the pain of others
Exhausted	God-strengthened
Forgetful	Organized
Forsaken	Concerned for the lonely
Grieving	Comforting
Impoverished	Hard-working
Impulsive	Spontaneous
Insecure	God-confident
Intimidated	God-dependent
Outspoken	Truthful
Overly sentimental	Sympathetic
Perfectionistic	Diligent, thorough
Physically frail	Understanding, kindhearted

Possessive	Loyal, dedicated
Quiet	Good listener
Reckless	Courageous
Rigid	Disciplined, decisive
Strong-willed	Persistent, determined
Slow learner	Attentive
Wasteful	Generous, bighearted
Wounded	Compassionate, sympathetic

Joanne and I are licensed facilitators for CORE STRENGTHS® (also known as SDI, Strength Deployment Inventory, a tool used by IBM, John Hopkins University, United Airlines, NASA, and many other groups). In CORE STRENGTHS®, they use the term "Overdone Strengths" to describe how a strength may be perceived as a weakness. For example: a strength of being "helpful" when overdone may be perceived by others as "smothering." When in conflict, the person who is analytical may become uncontrollably obsessive. When things are not going well, the competitive person may become in-your-face aggressive and domineering. Allow God to take control of your weakness because your core strength is often not far away.

One of Joanne's friends tends to get overwhelmed and anxious. She's sought the Lord in prayer, meditated on Scripture relating to anxiety, and received counseling. Accepting and acknowledging her weakness has strengthened her prayer life. Recognizing that an overloaded schedule increases her level of anxiety, she prays before accepting commitments and is careful to run things by her husband before agreeing to them. She's learned to live with margins in her life, allowing enough time for each activity or event. She practices daily balance—

sleep, exercise, healthy eating, meditation, and prayer. Her life exemplifies leveraging a weakness to become a stronger person.

Do Your Own Personal "SWOT"

A SWOT analysis is a strategic planning tool frequently used by businesses and organizations to identify internal and external factors that are favorable or unfavorable to reach objectives. SWOT stands for Strengths-Weaknesses-Opportunities-Threats.

Now, with the background of biblical strengths and weaknesses, you can do your own Personal SWOT. Using a blank sheet of paper, make a list of your Strengths and Weaknesses (identify weaknesses that you've identified as potential strengths from the list). Next, make a list of Opportunities and a separate list of Threats (challenges or seeming impossibilities). As Chuck Swindoll said, "We are all faced with a series of great opportunities brilliantly disguised as impossible situations."

TYPE THREE: PERSONAL SIN BENT

Stubbornness. An explosive temper. Addictive behavior. Uncontrolled lust. Self-centeredness. A judgmental or critical spirit. We can't escape this third form of weakness. It's called the sin nature, and we all have one. The apostle Paul struggled with his sin nature. "For what I am doing, I do not understand; for I am not practicing what I would like to do, but I am doing the very thing I hate" (Rom. 7:15). He adds his self-assessment of the turmoil within. "I know that nothing good dwells in me, that is, in my flesh; for the willing is present in me, but the doing of the good is not" (Rom. 7:18).

I've wondered why Paul didn't name the sin that caused him such great frustration. In all likelihood, it was too personal, perhaps embarrassing. I also think his many critics and foes could have used it against him. It's my hunch Paul's close companions knew the details and prayed for him in his struggle. The same may be true for you. There may be a sin weakness that isn't appropriate for you to broadcast to everyone, everywhere. Instead, confide in a close friend who understands and will be your prayer partner and hold you accountable.

Everyone has a unique vulnerability, an area where they're most susceptible. Some are wired with a hot temper and easily explode while others are so laid-back that blowing off steam isn't an issue. One person may struggle with addiction while another person has no desire for addictive substances but is prone to jealousy. Others struggle with lust and pornography while this isn't a temptation for someone else. Whatever it may be, your enemy knows it and targets you at your point of greatest vulnerability.

Our bents aren't necessarily sinful, but they may lead us into sin. Messiness—leaving the pizza box, chicken wings, socks, shoes, and newspaper strewn around the family room—isn't sinful *per se*. However, if this is an area of contention with your spouse, your response of insensitivity and stubbornness is sinful. In my opinion, watching a football game isn't sin, but watching football for nineteen hours over Thanksgiving weekend while neglecting time with God and family and shirking household duties is both a weakness and wrong.

We all come pre-designed with a sin bent, a tendency toward weakness. Which of the following do you struggle with? We'll discuss how to deal with these later in the chapter.

Common Sin Bents and Behaviors

Abusing others	Abusing yourself
Addictive behavior	Blaming, fault-finding

Complaining, whining	Conceited, self-important
Conniving, devious	Controlling, nagging
Critical, cutting	Deceitful, fraudulent
Demanding	Divisive, contentious
Drunkenness	Gluttony
Gossipy, nosy	Greedy, stingy
Lustful, immoral	Independent spirit
Jealousy, envy	Manipulating, using others
Materialism, idolatry	Needing to always be right
Occult activity	Pornography
Quarreling, disputing	Rebellious
Rude, insensitive	Resentful, bitter
Selfish ambition	Sexual immorality
Substance abuse	Swearing, profanity
Uncontrolled temper	Violent behavior

Sin leaves a trail of destruction, and it also distorts our thinking. I grew up looking into a distorted mirror—like a strange carnival mirror with a twisted picture—seeing my faults and flaws magnified and distorted. I acted out what I saw in the mirror. With God's forgiveness of my sins and by his grace, I began to look at a new mirror and learn healthier ways of thinking. Knowing God forgave me and totally accepted me reached deep into my shattered sense of worth and value. Christ's complete love and acceptance began to change my thoughts and responses. The new mirror reflecting these qualities began to change how I saw myself.

God's Mirror for Personal Confidence

◊ I am loved and accepted, completely and unconditionally (Isa. 54:10; Eph. 2:4; Rom. 15:7).

◊ I am forgiven, fully and repeatedly (Isa. 43:25; 1 John 1:9).

◊ I am blameless, without fault in God's presence (Eph. 1:4).

◊ I am God-designed, intricately and marvelously created (Ps. 139:13-14).

◊ I am valued, my life has meaning and purpose (1 Pet. 5:7; Ps. 138:8).

—Dave Beckwith

I put these on a card and began carrying them with me. God's Mirror for Personal Confidence began to change my sense of worth and value.

DAY TWO—CHAPTER TWO

TIME OUT

Power Thoughts for Your Time Alone With God

Knowing God forgave me and totally accepted me reached deep into my shattered sense of worth and value.

◊ Marvel as you read and reflect on God's love in Ephesians 1:3–14.

◊ Of the five phrases at the close of the chapter ("I am loved and accepted, forgiven, blameless, God-designed, and valued"), which one is the hardest for you to believe? Which ones help you the most with your sin bent?

◊ As you pray, reflect on the five statements in God's Mirror for Personal Confidence. Write them on a card and carry this with you to reflect on throughout the week.

TYPE FOUR: PERSONAL WEAKNESS DISGUISED AS A STRENGTH

At first glance, this type of weakness may seem perplexing. How can strengths be weaknesses? Does this diminish the value of strengths? Strengths, generally speaking, are a positive, but like any good gift, they can be misused or neglected. As weaknesses have positive potential, strengths also have the potential to be weaknesses. Before getting into potential misuse, let's begin with a brief look at strengths and gifts.

Knowing Your Strengths and Gifts

God designed everyone with a unique combination of strengths and weaknesses. While the focus of this chapter is on God's power being perfected in weakness, it's important not to overlook the flipside to the subject—your strengths. Discovering and engaging your strengths is important, and I recommend Strengths Finder, the popular Gallup assessment to detect your natural abilities and aptitudes.[7] Strengths Finder is available in twenty languages and has been used by more than ten million people in one hundred nations. The tool is a brief assessment and once completed, you'll receive a profile indicating your five areas of greatest aptitude. Examples of the assessment's talent themes include achiever, analytical, connectedness, consistency, empathy, futuristic, learner, and strategic to name a few of the thirty-four aptitudes.

As a believer, you've also been given a spiritual gift or gifts (usually more than one). These are different than natural strengths, but the two often work hand in hand. The New Testament has much to stay about spiritual gifts, but in brief, here are two important points. First: be knowledgeable about your spiritual gifts. Paul wrote, "Now concerning spiritual gifts, brethren, I do not want you to be unaware" (1 Cor. 12:1). For a

---

7. www.gallupstrengthscenter.com, accessed Sept. 7, 2019.

list of spiritual gifts, see Romans 12:6–8, Ephesians 4:11–12, 1 Corinthians 12:8–10, 28, and 1 Peter 4:9–11. Second: do not neglect to exercise your spiritual gifts. Peter wrote, "Each of you has been blessed with one of God's many wonderful gifts to be used in the service of others. So use your gift well" (1 Pet. 4:10 CEV). You may find it helpful to ask a mature believer to help you discover your gifts and how God can use you in exercising them.

Our natural strengths and spiritual gifts are from God. Think of them as treasures—in a positive manner as resources to bless others or negatively as sources of false pride. For the moment, let's compare your "strengths-gifts treasure" with "financial treasure." Money can be a great blessing to help others, or it can be a source of pride, hoarding, and self-sufficiency. Money itself isn't the problem—it's having a twisted attitude about money that creates the problem (1 Tim. 6:10). As money can be misused so can your strengths and spiritual gifts.

PREVENTING OVER-CONFIDENCE

Paul was a multi-talented, highly educated, fiercely driven achiever before coming to Christ. As he said, "Although I myself might have confidence even in the flesh. If anyone else has a mind to put confidence in the flesh, I far more:" (Phil. 3:4). Paul rose to the top; he was the best of the best. If he were in the military, he'd be a Navy Seal or a Green Beret. If he were in business, he'd be the CEO of a Fortune 500 company. Over-confidence was a real and present danger to Paul because of his background, education, and high level of achievement. To prevent himself from being over-confident, Paul intentionally put no confidence in the flesh (Phil. 3:3).

As mentioned earlier, weaknesses have positive potential, and strengths have the potential to be a weakness. Those with a high intellect may find they can coast and get good grades. By failing to achieve their potential, their strength becomes a weakness. The same can be said for those with exceptional athletic ability or a charming personality. Their strength allows them to slide by, and this tendency then becomes a weakness.

Several times I've asked an audience for a show of hands. "How many received honors as an athlete? How many were cheerleaders? Were any of you class presidents or a homecoming king or queen? How many received music or art awards or were honor students? How many have masters or doctorate degrees?" Hands go up, and I sincerely congratulate them on their achievements. I then point out these two verses as an encouragement to the large number of people who didn't raise their hand. "I don't see many of "the brightest and the best" among you, not many influential, not many from high-society families. Isn't it obvious that God deliberately chose men and women that the culture overlooks and exploits and abuses?" (1 Cor. 1:26–27 MSG).

If you've received honors and awards, this doesn't mean God can't use you. On the contrary, he'll use you greatly—but it may take a little longer. Why? God has to get you past relying on your accolades and awards.[8] Multi-talented believers may subtly congratulate themselves: *God, you're really fortunate to have me on your side. After all, I was an All-State basketball player, honor student, president of my class, and voted most likely to succeed.* And then God allows them to flounder and face one defeat after another. Why? God must bring them to the end of themselves. They must get acquainted with their weaknesses to experience God's power. After they're broken and have learned humility, God will use them greatly—but not until then.

Through the years, I've known a number of leaders with winsome personalities and exceptional speaking abilities.

8. I first heard this general thought in a message by Pastor Adrian Rogers, pastor of a Southern Baptist Church and President of the SBC Convention, at Bethel College's Founders Week, Jan. 23-26, 1984.

Relying on their natural gifts and with little preparation, they can get up in front of an audience and "wing it." Their strength becomes a weakness. They could be much more effective with preparation, and their pride stands in the way of their being greatly used by God. Subtly, they draw attention to themselves. Paul David Tripp says they become "very skilled self-swindlers."[9] I've also watched God set aside some of these highly gifted individuals—sometimes through failure—so they'd come to the end of themselves and start relying totally on Christ.

Surprisingly, Paul says this about his impeccable credentials: "Whatever things were gain to me, those things I have counted as loss for the sake of Christ. More than that, I count all things to be loss in view of the surpassing value of knowing Christ Jesus my Lord, for whom I have suffered the loss of all things, and count them but rubbish so that I may gain Christ," (Phil. 3:7-8). The word he uses for "rubbish" refers to trash, or more specifically, dung—cow manure. Paraphrased, Paul says, "The very credentials these people are waving around as something special, I'm tearing up and throwing out with the trash—along with everything else I used to take credit for" (Phil. 3:7 MSG).

Some assume Paul jumped up from his conversion on the Damascus Road and launched his first missionary journey. Not so. After surrendering his life to Christ, Paul spent three years in the desert of Arabia (Gal. 1:16-18), followed by eleven years serving Christ in relative obscurity. If Paul was thirty years of age when he came to Christ (which is likely, considering his training and accomplishments as a Pharisee), he didn't launch his first missionary journey until he was forty-four or forty-five years of age.

John Darby, a spiritual leader and Bible translator from the 1800s, said, "It is God's way to set people aside after their first start that self-confidence may die down. ... We must get to

---

9. Paul David Tripp, *Dangerous Calling* (Wheaton, IL: Crossway, 2012), 33.

know ourselves and that we have no strength."[10] This was the case for Paul and it was also true for Moses, who served forty years in Pharaoh's court followed by forty years tending sheep and getting his BD degree (Backside of the Desert degree). He was eighty years old when he began leading the children of Israel through the wilderness.

Often God "sets us aside" to give us time to understand our weaknesses and learn to serve in the power of the Spirit rather than the flesh. The antidote to "self-swindling" is to abandon our parade of self-righteousness and daily admit our life is a mess without continuous forgiveness, grace, and transformation.

If you're prone to charge ahead, relying on your natural abilities, keep serving—but slow down to recognize your weaknesses and acknowledge that you have no strength in yourself. Learn to wait on God. Listen to God and God's people. Be open to advice. Learn to value others. Allow your pride and stubbornness to be broken. Humble yourself before the Lord. "Get down on your knees before the Master; it's the only way you'll get on your feet" (James 4:10 MSG).

---

10. Stanford, *Principles of Spiritual Growth*, 11.

DAY THREE—CHAPTER TWO

TIME OUT

Power Thoughts for Your Time Alone With God

*It is God's way to set people aside after their first start that their
self-confidence may die down.
… We must learn to know ourselves and that we have no strength.
—John Darby*

◊ Read 1 Corinthians 1:25–31.

◊ What have been your proudest achievements? What
honors have you received? In what ways have these helped or
hindered you?

◊ As you seek God in prayer, ask him to show you the
difference between pride and humility.

1. When I'm proud, I'm confident in how much I
   know. When I'm humble, I'm aware of how much
   I need to learn.

2. When I'm proud, I harbor resentments and deny
   their effect on my attitude. When I'm humble, I
   choose to forgive others as Christ has forgiven me.

3. When I'm proud, I trust in myself. When I'm humble, I trust in God, knowing I'll certainly fail without his leading.

4. When I'm proud, I'm certain I don't need to change. When I'm humble, I daily admit my need for grace, forgiveness, and transformation.

5. Now add a few of your own …

WHY WEAKNESSES?

Most people have all four types of weaknesses, so don't assume you're the only one. In fact, Paul had all four types: 1) personal limitations—his thorn in the flesh; 2) personal woundedness—he got beat up a lot by his enemies, verbally and physically; 3) personal sin bent—he agonized over his sin bent in Romans 7; and 4) personal strengths that could have been his weaknesses had he relied on them.

To get a clear picture of why God designed us with weaknesses, let's focus on the classic verses on this topic.

> Because of the surpassing greatness of the revelations, for this reason, to keep me from exalting myself, there was given me a thorn in the flesh, a messenger of Satan to torment me—to keep me from exalting myself! Concerning this I implored the Lord three times that it might leave me. And He has said to me, "My grace is sufficient for you, for power is perfected in weakness." Most gladly, therefore, I will rather boast about my weaknesses, so that the power of Christ may dwell in me. Therefore I am well content with weaknesses, with insults, with distresses, with persecutions, with difficulties, for Christ's sake; for when I am weak, then I am strong. (2 Cor. 12:7-10)

In this passage, we discover answers to why God designed us with weaknesses and how he's using them to accomplish his purposes. Here is what God is teaching us through our inadequacies.

First, weaknesses keep you humble.

Have you been around people who think they're "perfection personified"? They put on a show of how smart, healthy, successful, and wealthy they are, subtly implying it's too bad you can't be flawless too. It's nauseating and phony. The Bible says, "First pride, then the crash—the bigger the ego, the harder the fall" (Prov. 16:18 MSG). In fact, I find it difficult to think of any sin that doesn't have pride at the root.

Instead, God wants us to have a proper perspective of ourselves. Paul used the phrase "to keep me from exalting myself" (2 Cor. 12:7). Because of the astounding revelations he had in the third heaven (2 Cor. 12:1-7), God used this "thorn in the flesh" to keep him humble.

Weaknesses are not about having a dinged-up self-image. God gives us incredible resources for a strong sense of worth: we're children of God; we're holy and blameless because of Christ; we have a personal friendship with the Creator. Now, so we don't waltz around thinking we're "little gods," God supplies us with a first-class set of weaknesses. As Romans 12:3 says, "Don't cherish exaggerated ideas of yourself or your importance but try to have a sane estimate of your capabilities" (PHILIPS NT).

SECOND, GOD USES WEAKNESSES TO BRING YOU TO THE END OF YOURSELF.

God encouraged Paul with these amazing words: "My grace is sufficient for you, for power is perfected in weakness" (2 Cor. 12:9). The word "sufficient" [Grk. word *arkeo*] means "to be satisfied, to be content." This is the same word translated "to be content" in Philippians 4:11–12. Paul never said, "I am content in whatever state I am in because I am a naturally contented person." No one is naturally contented. Instead, he said, "I have learned to be content, and I have learned the secret of being filled and going hungry" (Phil. 4:11–12).

Contentment is not learned when you have a ton of money and great success. You only want more. You'll never be able to fine-tune your life to achieve perfect contentment. Contentment is learned when you're exhausted, depleted—at your rope's end. You discover contentment when you come to the end of yourself. It is in these moments, when life turns difficult, that you discover the only source for contentment: JESUS PLUS NOTHING. *Being content (verb) has to do with your content (noun), Jesus living within you.* He is sufficient; he is all you need. Then, as we grow in Christ-centered contentment, we discover "godliness actually is a means of great gain when accompanied by contentment," and God "richly supplies us with all things to enjoy" (1 Tim. 6:6, 17).

God's grace is sufficient, and it is also extravagant. As Jack Miller said, "Cheer up! You're a worse sinner than you ever dared imagine, and you're more loved than you ever dared hope."[11] God's grace is forgiveness for your most grievous sin and sufficiency for your most difficult limitation. God's grace heals your personal woundedness, and his grace empowers you to forgive. The Christian life is grace upon grace and more grace … until we become grace-giving and gracious people. God's grace saves you, and his grace shapes you.

THIRD, WEAKNESSES AND BROKENNESS GIVE YOU A POWER EDGE TO BE USED BY GOD.

Look back again at 2 Corinthians 12:9–10. The words "weak, weakness, weaknesses" appear four times. This is the Greek word *astheneia,* a general word in the Bible for sickness, illness, or a lack of strength. Asthenia is a medical word in use today, meaning "the lack or loss of strength or energy, a sense of fatigue, or muscle weakness." In the field of psychiatry, asthenia refers to a lack of dynamic force in the personality or a fear of effort.[12] In a general sense, asthenia indicates a lack of strength, an inability to cope with life. Life's trials and troubles seem overwhelming. The frailty of astheneia may be physical, emotional, or mental.

Compare the word "weakness" with the word "power" or "strength," used three times in verses 9 and 10. The word "power" is the Greek word *dunamis* from which we derive the English

11. Jack Miller, www.goodreads.com/author/quotes, accessed Sept. 7, 2019.
12. *Mosby's Medical Dictionary,* 8th ed. (St. Louis: Elsevier, 2009).

word "dynamite" or "dynamic." As direct opposites, "weakness" is in sharp contrast to "power"—like comparing the fizz in a soda to the explosive power of dynamite.

Let's connect the two words—weakness and power. God made the earth and flung galaxies into place, and he created the mighty oceans and mountains. Nothing is greater than God's power. But how is this mighty power of God perfected? In verse 9, God says, "Power [Grk. *dunamis*] is perfected in weakness [Grk. *astheneia*]. The word "perfected" is the Greek word teleios (source of English words like telescope, telephone, television, telegenic, etc.), meaning "to bring something to completion, to fulfill an ultimate purpose." Here's the key: *God's awesome power, the power that creates and sustains the universe, is brought to its culmination, a crowning crescendo, a triumphant exclamation—in your daily weaknesses. Wow!*

FOURTH, GOD USES WEAKNESSES TO GET YOU READY FOR THE MAIN EVENT.

It's difficult to wrap our minds around this, but this life is not the main event. "You only go around once, so get all the gusto you can" is the attitude that permeates the thinking of most people. But that's faulty thinking. The main event is eternity and this life is preparation for "forever and forever." If we got healthier and stronger and better-looking every year, we'd never want to leave this life. Instead, as our bodies decline, God is preparing us to spend eternity with him in perfect, glorified bodies. Coming to terms with our weaknesses gives us an edge to live for the eternal. The Bible says this about the death of our human body: "It is sown in dishonor, it is raised in glory; it is sown in weakness, it is raised in power; it is sown a natural body, it is raised a spiritual body. If there is a natural body, there is also a spiritual body" (1 Cor. 15:43-44). I'm ready for my new body ... and the sooner, the better! How about you?

DAY FOUR—CHAPTER TWO

TIME OUT

Power Thoughts for Your Time Alone With God

*God's awesome power—the power that creates and sustains
the universe—is brought to its culmination, a crowning crescendo,
a triumphant exclamation—in your daily weaknesses.*

◊ Read 2 Corinthians 12:7–10 from these two versions to get the full impact.

Because of the surpassing greatness of the revelations, for this reason, to keep me from exalting myself, there was given me a thorn in the flesh, a messenger of Satan to torment me—to keep me from exalting myself! Concerning this I implored the Lord three times that it might leave me. And He has said to me, "My grace is sufficient for you, for power is perfected in weakness." Most gladly, therefore, I will rather boast about my weaknesses, so that the power of Christ may dwell in me. Therefore I am well content with weaknesses, with insults, with distresses, with persecutions, with difficulties, for Christ's sake; for when I am weak, then I am strong. (2 Cor. 12:7-10)

Because of the extravagance of those revelations, and so I wouldn't get a big head, I was given the gift of a handicap to keep me in constant touch with my limitations. Satan's angel did his best to get me down; what he in fact did was push me to my knees. No danger then of walking around high and mighty! At first I didn't think of it as a gift, and begged God to remove it. Three times I did that, and then he told me, "My grace is enough; it's all you need. My strength comes into its own in your weakness." Once I heard that, I was glad to let it happen. I quit focusing on the handicap and began appreciating the gift. It was a case of Christ's strength moving in on my weakness. Now I take limitations in stride, and with good cheer, these limitations that cut me down to size—abuse, accidents, opposition, bad breaks. I just let Christ take over! And so the weaker I get, the stronger I become. (2 Cor. 12:7-10 MSG)

◊ What weaknesses have been discouraging and difficult for you? In what ways have your weaknesses pushed you to your knees, so you don't walk around high and mighty?

◊ Ask God what he wants to accomplish in your life through your weaknesses.

HOW TO EXCHANGE WEAKNESS FOR STRENGTH

God's plan is to perfect his power in your weakness, so here's how to get started on your lifelong journey of turning weakness into strength.

FIRST, ACCEPT YOUR WEAKNESSES.

Paul said he was "well content" or he "took delight" in weaknesses (2 Cor. 12:10). Was he being masochistic? No. "Paul took no pleasure in the pain itself but rejoiced in the power of Christ that it revealed through him."[13]

God knows your weaknesses better than you do, and he has either designed them in your DNA or allowed them through your life experiences. God has been involved throughout the entire process. Even if you suffer deep scars from living in sin, God knows this, and he is ready to turn ashes into beauty. Now is the moment to take action: move from self-rejection and embarrassment at your weaknesses to accepting them. Take the time right now to pray:

> Thank you, Lord, for my personal limitations, woundedness, and sin bents. This is difficult to do because I have often wished I didn't have these things in my life, but now I realize you designed me this way, and you were overseeing each event in my life. I choose to accept these weaknesses, knowing you will display your power through them. Amen.

SECOND, APPLY GOD'S STRENGTH TO YOUR INADEQUACIES.

You may find yourself handling life quite well and suddenly circumstances come your way that hammer you hard. The bottom falls out: a friend turns against you, you're fired from

---

13. John MacArthur, "2 Cor. 12:10," *The MacArthur Study Bible* (Nashville: Thomas Nelson, 2006), 1752

your job, your teenager gets in trouble, your financial resources are wiped out, your house burns. Our friends, Pastor Larry and Faith Shelton, were living comfortably in Paradise, California. Larry served for eighteen years as senior pastor of the Paradise Alliance Church. After completing his ministry with the church, they decided to add on to their home creating a retreat center for pastors and missionaries. They had just completed this when on November 8, 2018 their home burned to the ground. They lost everything in the Paradise Camp Fire, the deadliest and most destructive wildfire in California history. The loss was overwhelming—and it didn't make much sense at the time. Nearly a year later, they are now discovering a bigger, more exciting picture of what God wants to do through them.

Paul affirmed twice that he didn't lose heart (2 Cor. 4:1, 16). Why? With enormous obstacles, painful persecution, physical limitations, mental anguish, and bitter opponents attacking him, what kept him going? What was his secret fuel? In 2 Corinthians, Paul lays bare his soul, stripping away any facade. Paul knew better than to pretend to be an all-sufficient tower of strength, a brilliant know-it-all. He often felt weak and inadequate. He leveraged every point of weakness to access the power of God. Triumphantly, he declared, "When I am weak, then I am strong."

Have you faced these life circumstances? After each question, I identify Paul's Power Principle—a paraphrase of how Paul, facing much the same pressure, appropriated God's power in his inadequacy.

Have you ever felt crushed and overwhelmed beyond your ability to endure? Did you feel your life was threatened? *Paul's Power Principle*: I was crushed and overwhelmed beyond my ability to endure. I thought I may never live through it. This drove me to stop relying on myself and to rely only on God who raises the dead (2 Cor. 1:8-9). When you are under great pressure, give up conniving, worrying, fretting, or manipulating the situation. Cast yourself completely on God and his power—power that raises the dead.

Do you sometimes feel unattractive or just plain ordinary, like a cracked clay pot? Do you worry about about making a good impression? *Paul's Power Principle*: When my body is fragile as a clay pot, and I feel quite unattractive, I remind myself that God displays his power in my feeble body—preventing anyone from confusing God's power as coming from me. (2 Cor. 4:7). Relax. Be yourself. After all, God made you, right? You don't have to be glamorous to glorify God. God's extraordinary power is displayed in ordinary people.

Do you feel inadequate, lacking confidence, or insufficiently qualified for the challenges in your life? *Paul's Power Pinciple*: When I was lacking confidence and feeling incompetent, rather than faking it, I relied on God, my source for competence and confidence. I didn't feel qualified to do anything on my own. My qualification comes from God (2 Cor. 3:4-6). Feelings of inadequacy are normal. Throughout the day, confidence levels will go up and down. There are moments when you'll feel totally inadequate. In prayer, draw on God as your source for competence and confidence.

Do you feel depleted, worn out, over-the-hill, lacking the strength to do what is required? *Paul's Power Principle*: I do not lose heart even though my outward body is growing weaker and decaying because my inner spirit is being renewed day by day (2 Cor. 4:16). God is glorified when we draw on his strength when we're exhausted or depleted. Isaiah said, "He [God] gives power to the weak and strength to the powerless. Even youths will become weak and tired, and young men will fall in exhaustion. But those who trust in the LORD will find new strength. They will soar high on wings like eagles. They will run and not grow weary. They will walk and not faint (Is. 40:29-31 NLT).

Are your financial resources minimal or depleted? *Paul's Power Principle*: I am poor, but I give spiritual riches to others. I own nothing, and yet I have everything (2 Cor. 6:10). You are a child of the King—infinitely wealthy in his resources. Though you may have little, rejoice in your bountiful riches in Christ.

Are you beat up, knocked down, confused and perplexed? *Paul's Power Principle*: I am pressed on every side by troubles, but I am not crushed. I am perplexed, but not driven to despair. I am being hunted down, but never abandoned by God. I get knocked down, but not knocked out. When I experience suffering, my body shares in the death of Jesus so the life of Jesus may be on display in me (2 Cor. 4:8-10).

Are you overwhelmed with sorrow? *Paul's Power Principle*: All praise to God, my merciful Father and source of all comfort. God comforts me in all my troubles so I can comfort others (2 Cor. 1:3-7). God is near to the brokenhearted (Ps. 34:18), and he heals the brokenhearted and bandages their wounds (Ps. 147:3). Pour your sorrow out to God. He understands and brings healing in his time.

THIRD, PLAY DEAD ... BECAUSE YOU ARE DEAD.

Regarding your sin bent, acknowledge that you're powerless to change your sin nature and its destructive, deceitful, arrogant ways. Realize God uses spiritual frustration and failure to turn you from trusting yourself to trusting in him. Your sin nature cannot be controlled, reformed, or improved by the noblest effort of human will-power.

When your sin nature is tantalized by a juicy temptation, play dead—because you are dead. "For you have died and your life is hidden with Christ in God. ... Therefore consider the members of your earthly body as dead to immorality, impurity, passion, evil desire, and greed, which amounts to idolatry" (Col. 3:3-5).

Sam is a believer who struggles with alcohol. His health is severely threatened, and he'll probably die from the effects of alcohol if he doesn't stop. Numerous times he's tried to have just one beer, but that stokes the fire for more. Eight to ten beers later, he's drunk and doing stupid things. He's aware of his sin and knows he needs to do something about it. Here's the advice I gave to him:

"Sam, before you die, you have to die."

"What?"

"Yes. The only solution to your problem with alcohol is to die to alcohol's power. Sam, have you ever met a dead person who's still dying for a drink?"

"No, I guess not."

"Does the desire for alcohol end at the point of death?"

"I haven't experienced that, but I reckon it does."

"So, Sam, this is what God wants you to do. Play dead because you are dead. When the temptation comes—and it will—rather than putting up a big fight to not have a drink, claim your position in Christ. Visualize yourself hanging on the cross, limp, lifeless, unresponsive. Hide yourself in Christ and reckon yourself to be dead. The temptation has no power over you when you claim your position in Christ." In addition, I urged him to participate in a recovery group and have a sponsor to check in with daily.

This is God's method to overcome the sin nature, and it works because it's the power of the cross. Paul exclaimed, "May it never be that I would boast, except in the cross of our Lord Jesus Christ, through which the world has been crucified to me, and I to the world" (Gal. 6:4). To boast in the cross is to be on the cross, crucified with Christ—"always carrying about in the body the dying of Jesus, so that the life of Jesus also may be manifested in our body" (2 Cor. 4:10). "Boasting in the cross" is essentially the same as "boasting in weakness," the next point.

FOURTH, BOAST ABOUT YOUR WEAKNESSES.

I admit this sounds strange. What did Paul mean when he said, "I will rather boast about my weaknesses, so that the power of Christ may dwell in me" (2 Cor. 12:9)?

Boasting about your weakness is not whining and complaining. This isn't an excuse to rehearse your aches and pains over-and-over again to the irritation of all who hear you. It isn't a martyr complex attempting to draw attention to yourself and your noble sacrifices.

Boasting about your weakness does not prohibit speaking of your accomplishments or credentials when appropriate. There is a danger of becoming a self-effacing person with a phony humility. When Paul confronted the boisterous, bragging false teachers, he went head-to-head with quite a list of his credentials and what he had gone through for the sake of Christ (2 Cor. 11:16-29). He concluded by saying, "If I have to boast, I will boast of what pertains to my weakness" (11:30). In the next chapter, Paul describes his experience of being caught up into paradise to receive direct revelation from God (2 Cor. 12:1–6). He follows this incredible credential with these words to the Corinthians: "I have become foolish; you yourselves compelled me. Actually I should have been commended by you, for in no respect was I inferior to the most eminent apostles, even though I am a nobody. The signs of a true apostle were performed among you with all perseverance, by signs and wonders and miracles" (2 Cor. 12:11–12).

There is a time to mention accomplishments and credentials but not for the purpose of boasting. The bottom line is this: "HE WHO BOASTS IS TO BOAST IN THE LORD. For it is not he who commends himself that is approved, but he whom the Lord commends" (2 Cor. 10:17–18).

Boasting about your weakness is an attitude of thankfulness, not complaining. The weakness may be painful,

79

perhaps the biggest trial of your life. Boasting about your weakness is giving thanks *in* all your circumstances (1 Thess. 5:18), not *for* all your circumstances. No one in their right mind is thankful they have cancer. But you can be thankful for God's grace giving you sustaining strength as you deal with cancer.

Boasting about your weakness is a willingness to be real, authentic. Pretending to be invincible is a great weakness; acknowledging weakness is a first step toward great strength. We may reason to ourselves, *I don't want others to know I'm struggling with this weakness. What will they think of me?* To prevent others from getting too close, we build a wall of independence and self-reliance. "Acknowledging weaknesses not only draws a person closer to God; it draws the person closer to other people. Weakness is the great leveler."[14]

One of my weaknesses is overeating. I admire people who can eat just two cookies. I start out with a baker's dozen. Some people are on a gluten-free diet, but I'm still working on a gluttony-free diet. I have a weakness for food—particularly if it's free. When I acknowledge my weakness and ask others to pray for me, I'm strengthened. This is an "advantageous edge" to keep from going over a "dangerous edge." My small group knows my weakness and helps keep me accountable.

Boasting about your weakness shines the spotlight on Jesus. Paul said he boasts about his weaknesses "so that the power of Christ may dwell in me" (2 Cor. 12:9). This phrase means Christ's power will be "a tent or a shelter" over you. Live in the tent of Christ's power over you. For example, if someone commends you for remaining calm in a heated situation. Respond by saying, "Thank you. It's possible only through Christ's power taking control over me. I'm capable of making a scene and saying things I'd regret later."

---

14. Jim & Betsy Gerrish, *The Word of God for Today*, www.wordofgodtoday.com/1-corinthians-13-2/, accessed May 5, 2019, s.v. "2 Corinthians 12."

FOURTH, ALLOW GOD TO CARE FOR OTHERS THROUGH YOUR WEAKNESS.

Who better to minister to someone with the loss of a limb, childhood abuse, unemployment, addiction, rejection, or loneliness than someone who's gone through the same experience? Out of your deepest hurt will come your greatest opportunity to help others. Paul said, "Who is weak without my feeling that weakness?" (2 Cor. 11:29 NLT). In your weakness, you'll have the opportunity to touch more lives than you ever imagined. God said, "My power works best in weakness," and Paul affirmed it: "When I am weak, then I am strong" (2 Cor. 12:9-10 NLT).

When Don Klassen, Joanne's cousin, was six years old, someone threw a bamboo stick that hit him in the left eye. His eye popped out of the socket and lay dangling on his cheek. Surgeons attempted to rescue the eye, but eventually they had to replace it with a glass eye (a plastic eye now). In Don's sensitive, formative years growing up, kids made fun of his glass eye, and girls said they couldn't handle being with someone with only one eye. Embarrassed, he had difficulty talking about his disability. Once he accepted his weakness, however, God began to use it in amazing ways. To overcome his lack of confidence, Don received training in public speaking. Today Don, married with three children and nine grandchildren, has had a unique ministry for several decades helping boys overcome their feelings of rejection. He is often asked to share his story with men's groups. God's power is magnified through a plastic eye and a humble man willing to tell his story.

VALUE IN AN OLD LAMP

While in junior high school woodshop, I made a lamp in the shape of a pump. Years later, I found it in storage. The wiring was frayed, the handle was broken, and the finish was scratched and defaced. My first thought was to dump it, but just before tossing it, my mind drifted back to woodshop and how proud I was when I brought that lamp home. Though it looked like a piece of junk, the value of that lamp was rekindled in my mind. I began to picture it repaired and refinished. In my spare time, I began working on that lamp—sanding, repairing, refinishing, and rewiring it. Today it's a treasured keepsake on my bedroom dresser.

The lamp didn't change itself. It only cooperated with the process. If the lamp jumped off the dresser and started talking— "Don't I look good? I did a pretty good job fixing myself up"— after I laughed myself silly and picked myself up off the floor, I'd be upset with the lamp's arrogance. Don't assume you're the one turning weakness into strength. God does the sanding, polishing, refinishing, and rewiring, and he is the power source.

I'm like that lamp, one toss away from the trash—faulty wiring, scarred finish, broken handle. And yet God values me. I'm his workmanship. He's patiently sanding, refinishing, rewiring, and changing me to reflect his light.

God made me, sin marred me, and Christ is mending me— from weakness to strength.

DAY FIVE—CHAPTER TWO

TIME OUT

Power Thoughts for Your Time Alone With God

Realize that God uses spiritual frustration and failure to turn you from trusting yourself to trusting in him.

◊ Read Colossians 3:1–10.

◊ Think about the last time you experienced spiritual frustration or failure. How did you respond? What was God teaching you?

◊ Have you tried "playing dead because you are dead" when you face temptation? Put this into practice this week when temptation comes knocking.

TIME TOGETHER

SESSION TWO

DISCOVERING POWER IN WEAKNESS

Is it a surprise that God's power works best when we're weak? Most Christians would like to experience more of God's power but have never seriously considered Paul's statement: "When I am weak, then I am strong" (2 Cor. 12:9). Let's get ready for an exciting session of discovering why God designed us with inadequacies and how he perfects his power through our limitations.

CONNECT

◊ Share a time when you felt particularly weak either physically, emotionally, or spiritually. What did you learn from that experience?

GROW

◊ Ask members of the group to read these passages aloud: 2 Corinthians 12:7–10, 2 Timothy 4:14–18, Romans 7:15–19, and Philippians 3:4–10. Pause after each passage to identify the weakness type and discuss examples, so everyone understands what's meant. Allow time for each person to identify one or more weaknesses in each area and share it if they're comfortable doing so.

1. Personal limitation

2. Personal woundedness

3. Personal sin bent

4. Personal weakness from a misused strength

◊ Discuss these two statements and how you've seen them to be true in your life.

1. "So I wouldn't get a big head, I was given the gift of a handicap to keep me in constant touch with my limitations. Satan's angel did his best to get me down; what he in fact did was push me to my knees. No danger then of walking around high and mighty!" (2 Cor. 12:7 MSG)

2. Until Paul accepted this limitation, Satan used it to discourage and defeat him. Once he was at peace with it, God uniquely displayed his power. The weakness became God's "power point"—a visual display of his power on the screen of Paul's life.

APPLY

◊ Discuss how you would apply these four steps to turn your weakness into strength.

1. Accept your weaknesses

2. Play dead because you are dead

3. Boast about your weaknesses (practice what you'd say about one of your weaknesses)

4. Allow God's power to be displayed through your weaknesses

◊ Read aloud in unison the "Changing My Mind" verse for this week.

Power Perfected in Weakness

"My grace is sufficient for you, for power is perfected in weakness." Most gladly, therefore, I will rather boast about my weaknesses, so that the power of Christ may dwell in me.

—2 Cor. 12:9 NASB

PRAY

◊ Give everyone a paper clip. In silence, unfold the paper clip, symbolizing the yielding of your personal limitations, woundedness, sin bents, and strengths to God. Then form the clip into a heart, symbolizing God's plan to take your weaknesses and make you strong for his glory. Hold the heart in your hand as the leader prays.

Prayer: "God, we thank you that we can come to you. You designed us with weaknesses and have allowed the experiences of life that have shaped us. We surrender our false sense of strength to you and admit how frail, weak, and needy we really are. Thank you for your acceptance, forgiveness, and your unconditional love. Like these paper clips, shape us into people who are strong, pliable, and usable for your kingdom, Amen."

◊ Optional: close with a song of worship (use a CD to sing with or have someone lead with an instrument).

SHARE

◊ This week be alert to people you meet who are exhausted, discouraged, or frustrated. Look for an opportunity to share an encouraging word or listen to them with compassion.

◊ Here are some thought-provoking questions that may ignite a discussion of God's strength and human weakness:

1. What is the toughest challenge you've ever faced? How did you handle it? Did you feel strong or weak when you faced this?

2. Where do you find strength when you're exhausted or feel hopeless?

3. What do you think of the statement "When I am weak, then I am strong"?

CHAPTER THREE

DEFUSING TORMENTORS IN THE MIND

Since your mind controls your behavior, let God control your mind and your behavior will change.

Our memory (or lack of it) makes for great humor. You've likely heard, "You no sooner get your face cleared up than your memory goes." Or, "The mind is a wonderful thing. It starts working the minute you're born and never stops until you get up to speak in public." Some joker said, "I'm not suffering from insanity. I'm enjoying every minute of it." In jest, I tell people who meet with me, "You can share your darkest secrets with me in absolute confidence. By tomorrow, I probably won't even remember who you are." Humor aside, our brains are amazing beyond comprehension.

During the 1956 US presidential campaign, a woman called out to candidate Adlai E. Stevenson, "Senator, you have the vote of every thinking person!" Stevenson shouted back, "That's not enough, madam, we need a majority!"[15] He had a great point: serious thinking about what we think and how it affects our lives is rare. Let's break out of that rut and do some serious thinking about thinking.

Transforming the mind is essential to discovering power in weakness. Memories, life experiences, and feelings affect our mental attitudes and behaviors. Sometimes bad memories play havoc with our thought life and leave us with weaknesses that sideline us. Even as a Christian, you may feel victimized and helpless, with negative thought patterns you can't shake. When you became a Christian, you received cleansing and forgiveness

---

15. One of the earlier references to this quote is in a book review article by Robert Sherrill in the *New York Times*, "Titles in the Running for 1972," February 13, 1972.

of your sins and a new life in Christ. But God doesn't hit FORMAT to delete all the gunk from your mental hard drive.

Millions worldwide are gripped with agonizing mental images that control their lives every minute of the day. Is it possible to break the chains of these mental tormentors?

◊ Scarring memories of a tragic accident

◊ Post-traumatic stress from war

◊ Shattered personal worth and lack of confidence

◊ Controlling compulsions and obsessions

◊ Attitudes of gloom, cynicism, and suicidal thoughts

◊ Memories of hundreds or perhaps thousands of pornographic images

◊ Scarring mental or physical abuse

◊ Memories of a past promiscuous lifestyle

◊ Uncontrollable fears and phobias

Here's the GOOD NEWS: God promises the human mind can be renewed—literally transformed from the inside out. These mental tormentors can be defused—rendered powerless. God's Word and the power of the Holy Spirit working in your mind will set you free. Like a virus scanner or defragmenter in a computer, God searches your mind to find and correct the areas that weaken your Christian faith. *Since your mind controls your behavior, let God control your mind and your behavior will change.* The process is amazing and supernatural, but not automatic. It requires an investment on your part.

Before digging into the "how to" for transforming the mind, let's start with an overview of current research regarding the wonders and astounding capacity of your mind. This information is crucial to better understand the process of transforming the mind.

YOUR NECK-TOP COMPUTER

Your mind is a powerhouse of potential, one of the most complex objects in the known universe. Though the brain is little more than the size of a large grapefruit, its capacity and versatility far surpass any computer in the world. This "God-designed neck-top computer" weighs in at about three pounds.

The component parts of your mind are staggering: "It is estimated that the brain contains more than one hundred billion nerve cells, which is about the number of stars in the Milky Way. Each nerve cell is connected to other nerve cells by thousands of individual connections between cells."[16] Some 100,000 miles of nerve fibers connect the various components of the mind.[17] In addition, the one hundred billion nerve cells, or neurons, connect with each other up to 60,000 times. And to think all of this fits into a size-seven hat![18] The signals of the brain are passed along at speeds up to 268 miles per hour. After each signal passes, it takes the filament about 1/2000 of a second to chemically recharge itself. At each firing, one nerve chemically communicates with another.[19]

If every person on the planet simultaneously made 200,000 phone calls, this would be the same total number of connections of the human brain in a single day.[20] Wow! Fearfully and

16. Daniel G. Amen, M.D., *Change Your Brain, Change Your Body* (New York: Harmony Books, 2010), 17.
17. Carl Zimmer, "Secrets of the Brain," *National Geographic*, vol. 225, no. 2, Feb. 2014, 37.
18. J. D. Ratcliff, "I Am Joe's Brain," *Reader's Digest* (April 1974), 91.
19. Ratcliff, 93.
20. *Human Brain: Amazing Facts*, May 13, 2010.

wonderfully made the Psalmist David exclaimed in astonishment at God's creation of the human mind and body (Ps. 139:14).

If family and friends chide you for having a one-track mind, take heart. They're wrong. You have two-tracks or two hemispheres in your brain, and you use both. "On the left, you have the talker, reader, speaker, writer, all-around deep-thinker. On the right, you'll find that music-lover, the deep-dreamer, the artsy type."[21] The left side is the analyzing, organizing, conceptual think-tank while the right brain specializes in feeling, touching, and empathy. The dominant side for most men is the left side while for women it's the right. However, everyone uses both the right and left sides of the brain, and both are continually in play.

A dense bundle of nerves known as the *corpus callosum* serves to connect your brain's right and left hemispheres. And a lively connection it is, with each of the 200-million nerve fibers in the corpus callosom firing a nerve impulse twenty times a second. Right now, 4 billion impulses are playing a game of high-speed ping-pong between your ears.[22] Next time you can't make it to work because of a throbbing headache, just tell your boss you're suffering from a corpus callosum right brain, left brain, high-speed ping-pong headache involving 200 million raw nerve fibers screaming between your ears.

In addition to left and right brain activity, memory consists of three types: working memory, short-term memory, and long-term memory.

WORKING MEMORY: YOUR COMPUTER SCREEN

Working memory is your immediate awareness, which fluctuates continually from one subject to another. "Working memory resides in the frontal lobe and lasts less than a minute. This form of memory is commonly referred to as one's attention

21. "Willard's Brain," *Campus Life* (September 1988), 40.
22. "Willard's Brain," 40.

span and lasts less than one minute before being erased."[23] Here the mind makes decisions, determines goals, interprets events, and acquires new beliefs, ideas, and opinions. The working memory perceives incoming information, interprets this information by comparing it with past data, and decides whether to act based on the incoming and stored information.

In fun I sometimes express my frustration, "These days I find myself thinking a lot about the hereafter ... I go from room to room in our house wondering what I am here after." It's more true than I like to admit. I go upstairs to get something ... my nail clipper, socks, shoe polish, or whatever. By the time I'm there, I'm wondering why I came upstairs. It makes me feel like I'm losing it, but in actuality, it's because working memory lasts less than minute—sometimes only fifteen to thirty seconds—unless it is rehearsed and reactivated.

Highly sophisticated equipment is now being used to peer into the brain and analyze its various functions and feelings. Colorized brain maps show different colors for different brain activities. Smell an onion; the brain lights up with a color. Pick up a dirty, smelly shirt, and the color changes. View a sunset or kiss your sweetheart, and the colors change again.

Mind-imaging was perfected long before the brain scanners of today. To the dismay of the Pharisees, Jesus, "knowing their thoughts" (Matt. 9:4), x-rayed their thoughts and photographed hidden brain activity. David recognized that God knew his thoughts from afar (Ps. 139:2). What if a mental scanner were developed that showed the thoughts of the person you were talking with? In turn, they could read your thoughts. Yikes! Mental hygiene would suddenly be the most popular self-help class. Thankfully, only Jesus has supernatural mind-reading ability. He knows your thoughts, even before you think them, ... and he loves you anyway.

23. Daniel G. Amen, M.D., *Change Your Brain, Change Your Body* (New York: Harmony Books, 2010), 237.

SHORT-TERM MEMORY:
YOUR RANDOM-ACCESS MEMORY

Throughout a day, we use our short-term memory for quick access to information we need. This is "… the material in the mind recallable by focusing attention upon it."[24] Short-term memory, as the name implies, resides inside the temporal lobes in an area called the "hippocampus"[25] and lasts a relatively short period of time before being erased. In some ways, short-term memory functions like a computer's random-access memory. Here you store phone numbers, the names of friends, your bank PIN number, and where you put your keys last night. Whoops! Can't find your keys? Here's why: the mental picture of the location for your keys slipped from your short-term memory.

---

24. John W. Drakeford, *Counseling for Church Leaders* (Nashville: Broadman Press, 1961), 16.
25. Daniel Amen, M.D., *Change Your Brain, Change Your Body*, 237.

DAY ONE—CHAPTER THREE

TIME OUT

Power Thoughts for Your Time Alone With God

Your mind is a powerhouse of potential, one of the most complex objects in the known universe.

◊ From your reading, what fact (or facts) about your brain "blows your mind"?

◊ Read Psalm 139:13–18 and thank God for your amazing mind. Make it your prayer of thanksgiving today.

◊ Why is random chance an inadequate explanation for the complex design of the human mind? Why does the complexity of the human mind argue for a designer with far greater intelligence?

◊ Go to the back of your book for this week's meditation verse titled "A Mental Makeover." Carry it with you or put it someplace where you can direct your thoughts to it throughout the day and memorize it.

Dave & Joanne Beckwith

LONG-TERM MEMORY:
YOUR HARD-DRIVE MEMORY STORAGE

Our minds contain a huge data bank somewhat like the hard drive of a computer. This is a vast storehouse of experiences, pieces of information, learned behaviors, and attitudes. By the age of seventy, it's estimated the long-term memory will file 100 trillion pieces of information. To put this into perspective, the *Encyclopedia Britannica* contains approximately 200 million bits of information.[26] This is equivalent to having 500,000 encyclopedia sets stored in your long-term memory. Over a lifetime, the brain erases some things to make room for new memories.

Long-term memory is a database that connects your past with your present. Along with facts and information, it also includes smells, sounds, tastes, and feelings available by recall: the color of the wallpaper in your mother's kitchen, the happiness of going fishing with your grandfather, feelings of being bullied at school, the rough edge of your dad's beard, the smell of fried chicken, etc. When you hear a church bell ringing, the mind will connect with that sound in your memory bank from some time in the past. When you smell cinnamon rolls, it may take you back to the warmth of your mother's kitchen. Or if someone speaks harshly, you'll connect with a moment in the past when someone spoke harshly to you. What's more, the feelings you felt then will surface and shape how you respond now. If someone explodes in a meeting over a trivial matter—a heated response entirely disproportionate to the issue—in most cases, there is a past experience that lit the fuse for the explosion.

What about repressed memories? This topic is controversial. Their was a surge of searching for unconscious memories during the 1980's. It was believed that when children were hurt—particularly with sexual abuse—they blocked out the memory to

26. "Willard's Brain," 40.

protect themselves from the pain. It was felt that recovering the memory would help adults overcome their current problems. Whenever someone had any of a wide variety of psychological symptoms, therapists were quick to view this as a hidden memory that needed recovery. After numerous studies, the American Psychological Association now states there is no verifiable information to this premise. When I speak of the tormentors in the mind, I am speaking of conscious memories.

Proverbs 12:8 speaks of the danger of a warped mind, and Romans 1:28 speaks of a depraved mind. Like your computer's hard drive, you can input perverse images as well as false data into your long-term memory. The brain's hard drive doesn't sort out what's true or false. As a result, your mind can be programmed with erroneous information, which nonetheless influences your decisions today. This vast data storage of experiences, pieces of information, learned behaviors, and feelings stored in long-term memory, affect behavior in the present.

What about subliminal influence? In 1957, an ad creator, James Vicary, claimed he increased sales of Coca-Cola and popcorn at a movie theater by flashing the words "Eat popcorn" and "Drink Coke" on the screen. The ads flashed by during the movie too quickly to be consciously noticed or spotted with the naked eye. Later, he admitted falsifying the results to gain attention for his business. Subliminal influence remains a debated topic with unproven results.

How about having an open mind? Yes and no. Proverbs 8:10 says, "My words are plain and clear to anyone with half a mind—if it is only open! My instruction is far more valuable than silver or gold" (TLB). On the other hand, many are proud of having an open mind—open to viewing, reading, or listening to anything, without discernment. The result is an open mind that needs to be closed for repair. Be open to fresh ideas, creative thinking, new ways of doing things, new research, and most of all, to the Word of God. Avoid distorted, perverse thinking, shameful input, gossip, off-color jokes, pornography, and the like—all are powerful in shaping your mind. What you allow to settle in the long-term memory will influence behavior and may come out under certain circumstances. Prior to death, while in an unconscious or delirious state, some begin to talk about information that's been buried in the long-term memory bank. This may be a frightening prospect, but here's the great news: *God can renovate and renew the long-term memory.* If this weren't possible, attempts at changing behavior would be futile.

During my seminary training at Talbot School of Theology, I developed an interest in the three different areas of the mind. I am thankful for the guidance of Norm Wright, psychologist, professor, and author, who directed my master's thesis which included this topic. I'm also grateful for the research and writing of Daniel Amen, M.D. and his help reviewing portions of this chapter.[27] His work includes brain imaging and diagnosis of former NFL players who suffered brain trauma in their careers. Dr. Amen has probably peered into more human brains than anyone in all of history, and he's one of the physicians who worked with Saddleback Church (Lake Forest, California) in the development of *The Daniel Plan*, a food and fitness biblical study.

The drawing that follows illustrates these three types of memory—though proportionately the long-term memory is much larger than illustrated.

---

27. Daniel Amen, M.D., *Change Your Brain, Change Your Body*, 8-9. For further study, Dr. Amen identifies different parts of the brain and how they affect behavior. The deep limbic system is the bonding and mood control center, the basal ganglia controls anxiety, panic, fearfulness, and conflict avoidance, the prefrontal cortex is the part of the brain that makes plans, controls impulses, and makes decisions, the singulate is the "gear shifter" that allows for moving from one thought to another, and the temporal lobes are involved with memory, facial recognition, and understanding language. Dr. Amen prescribes treatments for each region of the brain and how to deal with various issues such as anxiety, depression, ADD, obsessive behavior, and anger.

WORKING MEMORY

Computer Screen

Immediate awareness usually lasting less than a minute. Input for new information, ideas, interpreting events, and determining actions.

- -

SHORT-TERM MEMORY

Random Access Memory

Material in the mind recallable by focusing attention on it.

- -

LONG-TERM MEMORY

Hard Drive Memory

A vast storehouse of experiences, mental images, pieces of information, learned behaviors, and good as well as bad emotions. By the age of 70, it is estimated the long-term memory will file 100 trillion pieces of information equivalent to 500,000 encyclopedia sets.

Three Types of Memory

© 2015, Dave Beckwith

THE POWER TO CHANGE YOUR MIND

With an understanding of the amazing capacity of the mind and its power to affect our behavior, it makes sense to allow God to control your mind. Here are five steps to get started.

First, allow God's Word to do a deep scan of your mind.

The Bible says, "The Word of God is living and active and sharper than any two-edged sword (Grk. word *máchaira*), and piercing as far as the division of soul and spirit, of both joints and marrow, and able to judge the thoughts and intentions of the heart" (Heb. 4:12). The Word of God is compared to the sharp, two-edged sword, the *machaira*, used by soldiers in close combat. The double edges and sharp point changed the battle from the "cut and slash" of unwieldy, single-edged swords, six to eight feet in length, to the "stab and thrust" maneuver of a sword about two or three feet in length. Like the machaira, the Word of God delicately cuts and pierces deeper and deeper into your mind, penetrating through your outer facade and revealing what lies deep inside, even to thoughts you're unaware of. Everything is laid bare which may include mental tormentors like these:

◊ Resentful feelings

◊ Buried jealousies and anger

◊ Empty philosophies

◊ Anti-God thinking and attitudes

◊ Obsessions and compulsions

◊ Regrets

◊ Hatred, murderous thoughts

◊ Selfish motives

◊ Arrogance and cynicism

◊ Suicidal thoughts

◊ Pornography

◊ Sexually perverted images

◊ Fears and paranoia

What's stored in our inner being—the human heart and soul with the will, emotions, and thoughts—is who we are. This includes motives. Sometimes we're unaware of our motives or our motives are a jumbled mix of reasons for what we're doing. At other times, we have an ulterior motive—a concealed intent or purpose that differs from the stated or apparent reason. This is dangerous because our true motivation usually surfaces sooner or later. Solomon wrote about someone with ulterior motives. "Do not eat the bread of a selfish man, or desire his delicacies; for *as he thinks within himself, so he is*. He says to you, "Eat and drink!" But his heart is not with you" (Prov. 23:6-7 emphasis supplied). This verse affirms that we are what we think—even when we think we're fooling others. We may not be who we think we are, but we are what we think. This selfish person likely thinks of himself as a generous host providing delicious food and delicacies. However, his hidden motive is to take advantage of his guest. Deep inside, he is a self-centered person. Taking a hard look at our motives can be a revealing and sometimes horrifying experience. Allow the Holy Spirit to examine your motives and purify them. As much as possible, be transparent about your motives to others.

No person—not your spouse, not your best friend, not even you—knows all your thoughts. But God does. His scan sees all. "O LORD, you have examined my heart and know everything about me. You know when I sit down or stand up. You know my thoughts even when I'm far away. You see me when I travel and when I rest at home. You know everything I do. You know what I am going to say even before I say it, LORD. You go before me and follow me. You place your hand of blessing on my head. Such knowledge is too wonderful for me, too great for me to understand!" (Ps. 139:1–6 NLT).

What shows up on God's scan of your mind? Some of the thoughts may be cancer-like images that need surgery for your spiritual and mental health.

HOPE FOR MENTAL IMPAIRMENT

Most people know of someone suffering some form of mental impairment or reduced mental capacity. Caregivers often wonder, "How much do they understand? Are they capable of understanding spiritual truth?"

I knew Leona Gonzales for about twenty years as her pastor. She shared this remarkable story regarding her husband, Al.

Al was in the advanced stages of Alzheimer's. He would put his shirt and pants on over his pajamas, shave with a dry razor, and brush his teeth with VO5. He was unable to find different rooms in the house he built when we were married. He recognized me but did not recognize his own daughter or anyone else. Al had always loved working in the yard, but now he spent most of the day on the couch flipping through the TV Guide. I continued to pray that he would come to Christ before his earthly life was over.

One day, while Al and I were watching Nicky Cruz as he preached in the streets of New York, Nicky requested those listening to take the hand of the one next to us. Suddenly, Al was unusually alert, with an amazing mental clarity I had not seen for six years. We were seated at opposite ends of the couch, but he stretched his hand out to grasp mine. He was so intent on the message—his eyes glued to the TV set, and you could see he was lucid and really listening!

At the end of the message, Nicky Cruz asked us to repeat the sinner's prayer after him. Al did so ALOUD, hearing and repeating every phrase of the prayer! I was thrilled as I watched him. I asked him if he had prayed, and he said, "Yes, did you?" I said I had done it a long time ago. He said, "It wouldn't hurt for you to do it again." Even though Al's mind was ravaged with Alzheimer's, God granted a brief window of mental clarity as he understood the gospel, believed in his heart, and confessed faith in Christ with his mouth. Al became a new creation in Christ—new life despite a ravaging disease."

If you have a loved one suffering mental impairment, continue to pray that the Holy Spirit will speak to him or her. Tell the loved one often of God's love, read the Scriptures and play or sing hymns or praise songs with him or her. Often the mind, even with severe disease and loss of mental function, is capable of grasping more than we realize. The Word of God is powerful, penetrating to the division of soul and spirit.

Second, surrender mental strongholds.

The mind is a battleground. For example, you may be in the middle of a worship service at church, and an ugly resentment surfaces in your mind. Everyone is praising God, but you're consumed with seething bitterness and anger. Where did this come from? How do you deal with this mental stronghold?

Paul states, "The weapons of our warfare are not of the flesh, but divinely powerful for the destruction of fortresses. *We are* destroying speculations and every lofty thing raised up against the knowledge of God, and *we are* taking every thought captive to the obedience of Christ," (2 Cor. 10:4–5). The mental strongholds are fortresses, the "hide-outs" of destructive thoughts encountered during warfare with godless thinking. Contextually, Paul is talking about those who use speculations and lofty, arrogant words to attack the truth. The phrase "we are taking every thought captive" applies this warfare to the full realm of thought life—godless attacks on the truth from things you read and hear and from the fierce battle within your own mind. Camouflaged in secret strongholds, the negative thoughts—fiery darts of the enemy —are capable of vast destruction. From the fortresses in your mind, alarming thoughts may emerge—a seething bitterness, a lustful image, a painful put-down, a subtle jealousy, or a negative feeling.

You may wonder to yourself, *Why do I get these thoughts? If only I could stop thinking about ...* If someone says, "Do *not* think about yellow monkeys," what happens? Trying to not think about yellow monkeys makes it nearly impossible to stop thinking about yellow monkeys. Trying to suppress a thought simply doesn't work. What's the solution? Direct your thoughts to something else. The more you attempt to dismiss a negative, controlling thought, the stronger its grip. Turn your thoughts to a verse of Scripture or other positive thoughts.

Rather than trying to conquer mental strongholds in your own strength, take every thought captive to the control of Christ (2 Cor. 10:5). This is spiritual warfare. Imagine Jesus attacking a secret stronghold in the hills of your mind and doing combat with a sinister sniper. Following the battle, he chains the slimy thought and takes it captive. If the thought rears its ugly head again, claim the victory with a prayer: "Lord Jesus, this lust or resentment in my mind is tripping me up. I submit it to you. Take it captive, and by the power of your Word, render it ineffective in my short-term as well as my long-term memory. Amen."

DAY TWO—CHAPTER THREE

TIME OUT

Power Thoughts for Your Time Alone With God

God's power can renovate and renew the short-term and long-term memory.

◊ Return in your reading to Psalm 139. Today read verses 1-6 and 23–24. Make verse 23 your prayer today: "Search me, O God, and know my heart; try me and know my anxious thoughts."

◊ Ask God to point out to you what he sees on his scan of your mind: resentment, fear, jealousy, cynicism. Make some notes of mental areas to surrender as you allow him to take every thought captive.

Third, renew your mind.

With the surrender of your mental strongholds, you're ready for the transformation of your thought life giving you an edge over Satan's attacks. This is a key verse: "Therefore I urge you, brethren, by the mercies of God, to present your bodies a living and holy sacrifice, acceptable to God, which is your spiritual service of worship. And do not be conformed to this world, but be transformed by the renewing of your mind, so that you may prove what the will of God is, that which is good and acceptable and perfect" (Rom. 12:1-2).

At the start of this chapter, I set forth a simple principle: *since the mind controls your behavior, let God control your mind, and your behavior will change.* This is the simple truth of Romans 12:1–2. Verse one says: "… present your bodies [a once-for-all verb tense] a living and holy sacrifice, acceptable to God." Verse two is essential to apply verse one: "… be transformed by the renewing [a passive present tense verb, meaning a daily process] of your mind." God does the renewing as you change the input. My friend, Pastor Lou Damiani, compared "present your bodies" to a married couple offering themselves to each other on their wedding day, while the "renewing of your mind" is like the daily rekindling of the love relationship in married life.

The mind controls the body. Renewal transforms the mind. In practical terms, what does it mean to renew your mind? The word "renew" means to "renovate, refurbish, restore, to make fresh and new." During my college years, I worked part-time as a painter, refurbishing houses that, in some cases, had been repossessed by the bank. Prior to being evicted, some owners destroyed everything possible, beating holes in doors, pulling towel bars out of the walls, destroying the carpet, ripping appliances out and taking them with them. They were angry and bent on destruction. It took a lot of work to transform a beat-up house to look like a new one.

While Satan had control of your thought life, he filled your mind with destructive thoughts, sick attitudes, and stinking thinking. Now he's getting booted out. Before being evicted, he attempts to do as much destruction as possible. Since you've asked Jesus to take control and you're under new ownership, it's time to refurbish and renovate from the inside out.

Regardless of the perverse thoughts that have been stored or the bad attitudes that have gripped you, your mind can be changed. Here's the key: "Don't copy the behavior and customs of this world, but let God transform [the Grk. word is metamorpho] you into a new person by changing the way you think. Then you will learn to know God's will for you, which is good and pleasing and perfect (Rom. 12:2 NLT). Don't feed your mind the world's junk but be mentally transformed. The word metamorpho is not simply rearranging the furniture in your mind, tidying things up a little. It is a complete renovation, a radical and miraculous change. Not only *what* you think, but the *way* you think is changed. You develop a biblical worldview, a biblical value system that shapes your thoughts and behavior 24/7. The Greek word metamorpho is used only three times in the New Testament: Romans 12:2 and the following two passages. Notice the amazing transformation. "Six days later Jesus took Peter, James, and John, and led them up a high mountain to be alone. As the men watched, Jesus' appearance was transformed [Grk. word metamorpho] and his clothes became dazzling white, far whiter than any earthly bleach could ever make them" (Mark 9:2–3 NLT). "We all, with unveiled face, beholding as in a mirror the glory of the Lord, are being transformed (Grk. word metamorpho) into the same image from glory to glory, just as from the Lord, the Spirit" (2 Cor. 3:18).

Metamorphosis is the change of a worm-like caterpillar into one of God's most beautiful creatures, the butterfly. The 15,000 to 20,000 species of butterflies pass through what scientists consider to be a complete metamorphosis or four distinct stages: from an egg to the larva, then to a caterpillar, and finally, a butterfly. The crawling caterpillar is often a destroyer of plants and crops much like the out-of-control thoughts in your mind that produce destructive behavior. The change into a butterfly brings freedom, beauty, and wonder. Metamorphosis is the word God chose to describe the remarkable change he will perform in your mind.

THE BUTTERFLY AND YOUR PSYCHE

"The ancient Greeks believed that the soul left the body after death in the form of a butterfly. Their symbol for the soul was a butterfly-winged girl named Psyche."[28] While this is mythology, it is interesting that the Greek word for "soul" in the New Testament is the word psuche or "psyche," from which the word "psychology" is derived. In addition, Romans 12:2 uses the word that describes the change of a caterpillar into a butterfly (metamorphosis) for God's transformation of the mind. Your "soul" or "psyche" (your mind, will, and emotions) is being transformed from a caterpillar-like state into butterfly-like beauty by metamorphosis.

By the way, did you know the Bible is the greatest book in the world on psychology? It is a "soul book," with hundreds of references to the human soul. The Bible is filled with the greatest insights in the world regarding the human psyche or soul.

Renewing the mind involves changing the input and the content being viewed on the screen of your neck-top computer. Renewing is in the present tense (as previously noted), and this indicates a daily, ongoing process. When you became a believer,

---

28. *World Book Encyclopedia, 2007*, s.v. "butterfly."

you were given the "mind of Christ" (1 Cor. 2:16). This doesn't mean every thought you have as a Christian will be a Christ-like thought, nor does it mean you have a perfect perception of his will for every decision. There'd be no need for our minds to be renewed if we already had the totality of the mind of Christ. Properly understood, the mind of Christ is the enlightenment of Christ through the Holy Spirit to comprehend spiritual truth the natural mind cannot perceive.

Should a believer seek counseling or take medication as prescribed by a doctor? Yes. What is going on in the mind is spiritual, but it is also physical and mental. Biological chemicals—serotonin, dopamine, hormonal levels, etc.—are involved in the healthy function of the mind. When these chemicals are out of balance, the mind and emotions are greatly affected.

Take depression as an example. If you're living with unconfessed sin, you'll likely be depressed (Psalm 32). However, being depressed doesn't necessarily mean you have unconfessed sin in your life. Depression may be caused by the loss of a loved one, a disappointing setback, buried anger, or a variety of other factors. Counseling will help process these feelings. Depression may also be biological—thyroid dysfunction, illness or disease, chemical imbalance, and a wide variety of other causes. The body, the soul (the thoughts of the mind, will, and emotions), and the spirit are interrelated, with each impacting the other. Being such close neighbors, when one catches something, it affects the others. Effective diagnosis and treatment are always holistic, examining the physical, mental, emotional, and spiritual.

DAY THREE—CHAPTER THREE

TIME OUT

Power Thoughts for Your Time Alone With God

The process of bringing information from the short-term memory to the screen of your mind and reflecting on it is called meditation— the key to renewing your mind.

◊ Read Romans 12:1–2 in your Bible and then compare it to this paraphrase.

> So here's what I want you to do, God helping you: Take your everyday, ordinary life—your sleeping, eating, going-to-work, and walking-around life—and place it before God as an offering. Embracing what God does for you is the best thing you can do for him. Don't become so well-adjusted to your culture that you fit into it without even thinking. Instead, fix your attention on God. You'll be changed from the inside out. Readily recognize what he wants from you, and quickly respond to it. Unlike the culture around you, always dragging you down to its level of immaturity, God brings the best out of you, develops well-formed maturity in you. (Rom. 12:1-2 MSG)

◊ Sit at your kitchen table and place a mug on the table in front of you and one across from you. Enjoy a beverage and treat if you'd like. Now settle in to have a conversation with Jesus. I encourage you to talk out loud if you feel the freedom to do so. Read Romans 12:1–2, slowly and thoughtfully reflecting on each phrase. During your conversation with Jesus, discuss these thoughts with him.

1. When did you first offer or present your body to him?

2. What joy did this bring to you?

3. What have been the struggles to stay committed?

4. Tell him about the pressures around you to conform to the thoughts of the world.

5. What is his plan for you to renew your mind?

6. Ask him to help you respond to his nudging.

7. Visualize the impact on your life when your mind is transformed.

8. Thank him for what he will do.

FOURTH, DEVELOP A PLAN FOR DAILY MEDITATION.

I'm skeptical when someone tells of some secret formula that guarantees success. But when God says, "Do this, and you will be successful," I'm tuned in. Many people think prosperity and success come from having power and money, a winning attitude, influential personal contacts, working long hours, and a relentless desire to get ahead. Instead, God promises success for the person who develops and cultivates a simple practice: meditation. This is the success edge to win in this high-pressure, intimidating world.

> Be strong and courageous, for you are the one who will lead these people to possess all the land I swore to their ancestors I would give them. Be strong and very courageous. Be careful to obey all the instructions Moses gave you. Do not deviate from them, turning either to the right or to the left. Then you will be successful in everything you do. Study this Book of Instruction continually. Meditate on it day and night so you will be sure to obey everything written in it. Only then will you prosper and succeed in all you do. This is my command—be

strong and courageous! Do not be afraid or discouraged. For the LORD your God is with you wherever you go. (Josh. 1:6–9 NLT)

My hunch is that Joshua was shaking in his sandals as he stepped into the leadership role vacated by the great leader Moses. How do you follow a leader who God used to humble the most powerful nation of the day by calling down supernatural plagues, a leader who carried a big stick that split the Red Sea, a leader who came down from a mountain with the Ten Commandments directly from God, a leader who struck a rock and water poured forth, and a leader who spoke directly with God on a regular basis? Joshua also faced the daunting task of conquering thirty-one kings in the battles for the promised land.

Joshua had every reason to be intimidated. God knew this, so he gave Joshua the resource to overcome intimidation. Look at Joshua 1:6–9 and underline the three times the phrase "be strong and very courageous" appears. Feeling inadequate and intimidated are common weaknesses. What changes inadequacy into strength and intimidation into courage? *Biblical meditation is intimidation medication.*

What is meditation? Many think of meditation as something monks do isolated from people while sitting on a hillside eating bird seed. Others associate meditation with various forms of eastern mysticism—emptying the mind while sitting cross-legged on a rug in a semi-trance. This is *not* biblical meditation. An empty mind is a vulnerable mind. Never does the Bible tell us to empty our minds. J. I. Packer, writing in his classic work *Knowing God*, says, "Meditation is the activity of calling to mind, and thinking over, and dwelling on, and applying to oneself, the various things that one knows about the works and ways and purposes and promises of God. It is an activity of holy thought, consciously performed in the presence of God, under the eye of God, by the help of God, as a means of communion with God."[29]

Below, stated briefly, is my summation of why developing the practice of meditation will have such a great impact on your life.

Biblical Meditation ...

... isn't emptying your mind; it's filling your mind with God.

... doesn't require isolation; it fits with the flow of your busy life.

... doesn't complicate your life; it's your compass in the midst of chaos.

... overcomes intimidation with God-courage (Josh. 1:6–9).

... builds strong faith (Rom. 10:17).

... will help you overcome temptation (Ps. 119:11).

... is God's prescription to heal your mind and emotions (Rom. 12:1–2).

... is an effective antidote to worry (Phil. 4:6–8).

... changes your attitude and outlook on life (Phil. 4:7).

... brings success to your endeavors (Ps. 1:2-3).

... is the key to perfect peace (Isa. 26:3).

Nicholas Carr, in his book titled *The Shallows: What the Internet Is Doing to Our Brains*, contends that the internet has

---

29. J. I. Packer, *Knowing God* (Downers Grove, IL: InterVarsity Press, 1973), 18–19.

brought a drought of deep thinking and ability to concentrate on a subject. He affirms the many benefits of the internet— banking, real-time news, shopping, research, communication, email—but laments that the more time we spend on the web, jumping from one site to another, the more incapable we become at concentrating. We lose the ability to think deeply about a subject. Biblical meditation refocuses the working mind over-and-over again to a singular thought or verse, allowing it to be analyzed, amplified, and applied. It is like holding a sparkling diamond up to the light and seeing it from every angle possible. Biblical meditation is a return to deep thinking about God and eternal issues.

Scripture memorization is a wonderful way to retain God's Word and have it available whenever you need it. The Psalmist wrote, "I have hidden your word in my heart, that I might not sin against you" (Ps. 119:11 NLT). However, many people have a "mental block" regarding memorizing and quickly protest, "I can't even remember someone's name." I was surprised to discover the words "memorize" and "memorization" are not found in the Bible even though Jewish training included memorizing Scripture, and memorization is implied in Psalm 119:11. Instead, the Bible frequently uses the word "meditate." Personally, I've memorized many verses by repeatedly meditating on them. The by-product of repeated meditation is memorization, and memorization helps facilitate meditation. Focus on daily meditation, and you'll be surprised how easy it is to memorize the verse. Carry a verse with you for a week, think about it throughout the day, and by the end of the week, you will be able to recite it from memory. Because of God's emphasis on Scripture meditation, I believe this is the key to transforming the mind and changing behavior. Yes, I recommend memorizing Scripture, but use meditation as the process to facilitate memorization. As you continue doing this, your long-term memory will be filled with the Word of God, the key to transforming your mind.

Closely associated with meditating on God's Word is the word "delight"—a word found nine times in Psalm 119, the great chapter on biblical meditation. The Hebrew word for "delight" means "to sport, to play with, to take delight in." If you're excited about the purchase of a new electronic gadget, you take delight in it by playing with it, fiddling around with it, discovering all its features. The best way to grasp the "how to" for the electronic gadget is to have fun with it. If you approach it as drudgery, learning it will be much more difficult. Educators affirm that the most effective learning is fun, not a laborious grind. While I'm not suggesting manipulating the meaning of a verse, when you meditate on Scripture, take delight in it, play with it in your mind, think about it in new and interesting ways, analyze it, amplify it, apply it, pray about it, sing about it, rejoice in it, and even dance to it. David said, "I dance to the tune of your revelation" (Ps. 119:70 MSG), an interesting paraphrase of "I delight in your instructions" (NLT). Enjoying the music of meditating will strengthen you as you walk through tough times: "If your revelation hadn't delighted me so, I would have given up when the hard times came" (Ps. 119:92 MSG). While meditation doesn't require isolation, it's helpful to have moments when you get alone for fifteen to twenty minutes or more to meditate.

Daily meditating on the thoughts of God makes it easy to "talk it through" with the family in teachable moments during the day. "These words, which I am commanding you today, shall be on your heart. You shall teach them diligently to your sons and shall talk of them when you sit in your house and when you walk by the way and when you lie down and when you rise up. You shall bind them as a sign on your hand and they shall be as frontals on your forehead. You shall write them on the doorposts of your house and on your gates" (Deut. 6:6–9).

More than reading a verse in the morning, allow God's Word to saturate your thoughts throughout the day. Learn to think biblically. Put verses on the refrigerator, the bathroom mirror, your computer screen, or your desk at work. Tuck verse cards with the napkin holder so you can talk about them during the evening meal. Bible software is available for your computer as well as other electronic devices. I have nine versions of the Bible on my cell phone, and I'll often flip it open to read a few verses while I'm waiting in line. As a teenager, I memorized all the verses in the *Topical Memory System* developed by the Navigators. AWANA is a wonderful program to get your children started memorizing and valuing Scripture. The Bible is also available on CDs or DVDs. Use your commute time to listen to CDs or tune in your radio to some excellent Christian teaching. It will transform your mind and change your life!

Never have there been more resources to enable biblical meditation—and never have there been more distractions to interfere with practicing biblical meditation. Make it a top priority.

DAY FOUR—CHAPTER THREE

TIME OUT

Power Thoughts for Your Time Alone With God

Biblical meditation refocuses the working mind over-and-over again to a singular thought or verse, allowing it to be analyzed, amplified, and applied. It is like holding a sparkling diamond up to the light and seeing it from every angle possible.

◊ To practice meditation, ask God to speak to your heart, and then read a passage of Scripture (use more than one translation if available). After reading it, go back and take it phrase by phrase, mentally "chewing on" on each key thought. What does this mean in practical terms? How do I apply this to my life? Then pray the thoughts of the passage back to God using your own words. You may choose to stay in one passage for a day or even a week. Allow the passage to become part of who you are.

◊ Now let's practice biblical meditation. Read Psalm 1:1–3 in your Bible and then compare it to the paraphrase below.

Oh, the joys of those who do not follow evil men's advice, who do not hang around with sinners, scoffing at the things of God. But they delight in doing everything God wants them to, and day and night are always meditating on his laws and thinking about ways to follow him more closely. They are like trees along a riverbank bearing luscious fruit each season without fail. Their leaves shall never wither, and all they do shall prosper. (Ps. 1:1–3 TLB)

FIFTH, GUARD YOUR MIND.

"Be careful what you think, because your thoughts run your life" (Prov. 4:23 NCV). What a sobering thought. Your life can run amuck or succeed depending on what goes on between your ears. The computer world uses the phrase, "Beware of GIGO." This means "garbage in, garbage out," and this is true for your God-designed neck-top computer as well.

Solomon, in a man-to-man talk with his sons, warned, "Above all else, guard your affections. For they influence everything else in your life: ... Look straight ahead; don't even turn your head to look" (Prov. 4:23, 25 TLB). He was talking about the danger of a sensual woman. The visual cortex is more active in men than in women. As a result, pornographic images get a stronger grip on the mind of a man. Most men find it difficult to look away from a pornographic image because their mental receiver locks into the strong visual signal. William Struthers in *Wired for Intimacy: How Pornography Hijacks the Male Brain* says, "As men fall deeper into the mental habit of fixating on sexual images, the exposure to them creates neural pathways. With each lingering stare, pornography deepens a Grand Canyon-like gorge in the brain through which images of women are destined to flow."[30] Chemicals released in the neural pathways of the brain lead to a rewiring that is similar to drug addiction, causing the viewer to need more. Clay Olsen, executive director of Fight the New Drug, says, "Studies have shown that individuals who regularly consume pornography can end up preferring the computer screen to a human being to get their sexual fix."[31] What goes on in the mind will affect behavior sooner or later. Conversely, when behavior is acted out, it creates a neural pathway in the brain, which in turn reinforces the behavior. Paul warned about

30. William M. Struthers, *Wired for Intimacy: How Pornography Hijacks the Male Brain* (Downers Grove, IL: InterVarsity Press, 2009), 85, 106.
31. "Porn: the New Drug," *afaJournal*, Oct. 2014, Vol. 38, No. 9, 4

the grip of sexual sin and confirmed that sinning without restraint yields a depraved mind. "God gave them over to a depraved mind, to do those things which are not proper, being filled with all unrighteousness, wickedness, greed, evil; full of envy, murder, strife, deceit, malice; *they are* gossips, slanderers, haters of God, insolent, arrogant, boastful, inventors of evil, disobedient to parents, without understanding, untrustworthy, unloving, unmerciful;" (Rom. 1:28–31).

The good news is that healthy mental patterns and sexual appetites can be reestablished by intentionally redirecting the neurochemical flow and renewing the mind in the Word of God. Thought patterns and behavior are inseparable. For this reason, guard your mind as if it were Ft. Knox, the heavily fortified U.S. Mint depository for bullion deposits and gold reserves.

However, I don't recommend isolating from the world or cutting off all awareness of current events. To maintain a perspective on world events, I read several magazines, including *Time*, *World*, *Christianity Today*, *Decision*, and several others. My friend and long-time mentor, Dr. George Cowan, President Emeritus of Wycliffe Bible Translators, along with his wife, Florie, combined prayer with watching the evening news. Together they would view a report of developments in some part of the world. When the commercial came on, they hit the mute button and prayed for that area of the world. They knew missionaries in nearly every part of the world, so they prayed specifically for them by name.

How do you choose content that is acceptable in a movie, book, or television show? First, check the internet to review the content and ratings in advance. Next, be sensitive to how it may affect others, especially children. My wife reacts differently than I do to watching an intense, suspenseful program. I've learned to check with her before assuming she wants to see a particular program. We stop a movie after only a few minutes if we feel the content is inappropriate or if the movie looks like a senseless waste of time.

It is a fact that the Bible has some violent scenes (check out the book of Judges), and sexuality is presented in appropriate detail in several places. Some parts of the Bible would likely be rated at least PG-13 if not R. But why is the content in the Bible, even when it describes immoral or violent scenes, different from much of today's media content? With biblical content, God is God, sin is sin, right and wrong have consequences, truth is not relative, and morality is clear. In today's media, blurred morality is a dangerous and subtle form of indoctrination. Sex outside of marriage is taken for granted: "Hey, everybody's doing it, so what's wrong with you?" Profanity and cursing are commonplace. Right and wrong are mocked, while tolerance of sin is applauded. Cheating is okay if you can get away with it. Anti-God thinking is subtly introduced and woven into the tapestry of a media-distorted worldview.

Has it always been this way? On December 6, 1951, the National Association of Broadcasters enacted a Television Code that governed the content of TV. It blended the codes of the three networks—ABC, CBS, and NBC—in an attempt to prevent government regulation. Nearly all US television programs from 1952 through the early 1980s complied with the code, and this was indicated by the Seal of Good Practice in the closing credits. What was in the code?

> The code prohibited the use of profanity, the negative portrayal of family life, irreverence for God and religion, illicit sex, drunkenness and addiction, presentation of cruelty, detailed techniques of crime, the use of horror for its own sake, and the negative portrayal of law enforcement officials, among others. The code regulated how performers should dress and move to be within the "bounds of decency." Further, news reporting was to be "factual, fair and without bias" and

commentary and analysis should be "clearly defined as such."[32]

The code was revised several times before being suspended in 1983 due to a settlement with the Justice Department. Here are some of the moral and ethical standards from the Code of Practices for Television Broadcasters, with the section and paragraph indicated (the headings are supplied).

Language: (a) Profanity, obscenity, smut and vulgarity are forbidden, even when likely to be understood only by part of the audience.

Faith: (b) Attacks on religion and religious faiths are not allowed. Reverence is to mark any mention of God, his attributes and powers.

Marriage and divorce: (d) Respect is maintained for the sanctity of marriage and the value of the home. Divorce is not treated casually nor justified as a solution for marital problems."

Sex and nudity: (e) Illicit sex relations are not treated as commendable. (f) Sex crimes and abnormalities are generally unacceptable as program material. From the section on "Decency and Decorum in Production": (1) The costuming of all performers shall be within the bounds of propriety and shall avoid such exposure or such emphasis on anatomical detail as would embarrass or offend home viewers.

Substance abuse: (g) Drunkenness and narcotic addiction are never presented as desirable or prevalent.

Occult: (l) Exhibitions of fortune-telling, astrology ... palm-reading, and numerology are acceptable only when required by a plot of the theme of a program, and then the presentation should be developed in a manner designed not to foster superstition or excite interest of belief in these subjects.

---

32. "Code of Practices for Television Broadcasters "Television History - The First 75 Years," *Wikipedia Encyclopedia*.

Crime: (q) Criminality shall be presented as undesirable and unsympathetic. The condoning of crime and the treatment of the commission of crime in a frivolous, cynical or callous manner is unacceptable.

Horror: (s) The use of horror for its own sake will be eliminated; the use of visual or aural effects which would shock or alarm the viewer, and the detailed presentation of brutality or physical agony by sight or by sound are not permissible.

A lot has changed—the standards of decency have nose-dived. Little by little, we've grown accustomed to what we considered unacceptable a few decades ago. "The regulations for content laid down by the Television Code almost sound quaint by modern standards, but they provide a startling glimpse into how much our culture has changed in the past 50 years."[33] No one would dare call it brainwashing (after all, we do have a choice in what we view), but we've grown quite comfortable being conformed to the world rather than being transformed by renewing our minds with the thoughts of God (Rom. 12:2).

Allow the Holy Spirit to guide you in the development of your personal standards to guard your mind. "Changing Channels on My Mind," which follows, is a grid to check the content of movies or television. Be courageous and willing for the Holy Spirit to check what you feed your mind.

---

33. Ed Vitagliano, "TV's fall," *afaJournal,* vol. 38, no. 8, Sept. 2014.

CHANGING CHANNELS ON MY MIND

"Fix your thoughts on what is true, and honorable, and right, and pure, and lovely, and admirable. Think about things that are excellent and worthy of praise" (Phil. 4:8 NLT). Here is a grid to check movies, television, internet, and books before allowing them to invade your mind.

Positive Values

Does the TV program, movie, internet media, or book focus on values such as these?

◊ Truth (accurate portrayal of right and wrong, informative, provides a window to learn and better understand the world, does not distort God's truth)

◊ Excellence (uplifting, valuable, worthwhile)

◊ Kindness (compassion, tenderness, gentleness, value for people)

◊ Family Values (morally uplifting, clear standards of right and wrong)

◊ Humor (clean jokes and situational comedy)

◊ Respect (authority is honored: God, government, police, schools, and parents)

◊ Faith (God is recognized as the giver and sustainer of life; religious life and personal belief are respected)

◊ Other: _____

Negative Values

Does the TV program, movie, internet, or book glamorize and encourage these behaviors? Are they practiced without consequences, applauded as normal, or presented in enticing ways?

◊ Immorality (sexual language or scenes, sex outside of marriage, nudity, etc.)

◊ Profanity (swearing, foul, or abusive language)

◊ Violence (murder, abuse, rape, etc.)

◊ Rebellion (defiance of God)

◊ Occult (astrology, witchcraft, sorcery, occult)

◊ Greed (materialism, drugs, gluttony, self-indulgence)

◊ Other: _____

Note: It is very difficult to find content on TV or in the movies that does not have some of the negative values above. In fact, the Bible presents stories and descriptions of the negative but in appropriate ways. The key has to do with how the negative is presented and how it affects your mind. Guard against the portrayal of negative values in a way that glorifies sinful behavior and colors your thinking in perverted ways.

Be clear about your own choices, but guard against being legalistic in imposing your standards on others. Allow the Holy Spirit to direct your life as well as theirs. In other words, don't play Holy Spirit in another person's life. Whether you're watching TV, talking with a friend, choosing a movie, or surfing the web, ask yourself this: Are my thoughts pleasing to God? Is Jesus comfortable viewing the screen of my mind with me? Join the Psalmist David in praying, "May the words of my mouth and the meditation of my heart be pleasing to you, O Lord, my rock and my redeemer" (Ps. 19:14 NLT).

TRANSFORMATION OF YOUR MIND: WHAT TO EXPECT

When you cooperate with God in consistently renewing your mind over a period of time, God promises metamorphosis, worm-to-butterfly transformation. But what is happening in your long-term memory, your mental hard drive? Do memories of rejection, jealousy, or lustful thoughts disappear? Does the memory of a tragic accident vanish? Do you forget being abused as a child? I acknowledge that I don't fully understand the process, but I testify that God is transforming my mind—healing the scars of rejection, abuse, perverse images, and a distorted view of myself. Here are four aspects of what to expect when God transforms your mind.

First, mental metamorphosis changes the content of your mind.

As God's Word enters your mind, it is first displayed on the screen of your working memory before being stored in your short-term and long-term memory. As you meditate on

Scripture, you bring it from the short-term memory to the working memory over and over again. The more you repeat this process, the greater the impact. The input of God's Word into your mind works to change the output—your attitudes and thinking followed by your actions.

Input

For the word of God is alive and powerful. It is sharper than the sharpest two-edged sword, cutting between soul and spirit, between joint and marrow. It exposes our innermost thoughts and desires. (Heb. 4:12 NLT)

Output

Do not be conformed to this world, but be transformed by the renewing of your mind. (Rom. 12:2 NASB)
You will keep in perfect peace all who trust in you, all whose thoughts are fixed on you! (Is. 26:3 NLT)

WORKING MEMORY
Computer Screen

Fix your thoughts on what is true, and honorable, and right, and pure, and lovely, and admirable. Think about things that are excellent and worthy of praise. (Phil. 4:8 NLT)

SHORT-TERM MEMORY
Random Access Memory

I have hidden your word in my heart that I might not sin against you. (Ps. 119:11 NIV)

LONG-TERM MEMORY
Hard Drive Memory

Take captive every thought to make it obedient to Christ. (2 Cor. 10:5 NIV)

Jealousies   Hatred   Pornographic Images   Fetishes

Cynical Thinking   Resentments   Rage   Abuse

Controlling Fears   Gloom   Regrets

Changing Your Mind

© 2015, Dave Beckwith

This is rock-solid biblical truth. The Word of God penetrates like a two-edged sword into the depths of your inner thought life, exposing the mental images, memories, and attitudes of the heart (Heb. 4:12–13). God works within your mind to demolish mental strongholds as you take every thought captive in obedience to Christ (2 Cor. 10:3–5). This reminds us that the mind will always be a battleground. Temptations come via our thoughts, which must be continually surrendered to Christ. As you renew your mind, God transforms it by the power of his Word (Rom. 12:2).

With the input of the Word of God into your mind, it overwrites and defuses the negative buried in your long-term memory: jealousies, hatred, pornographic images, cynical thinking, put downs, resentments, rage, abuse, controlling fears, gloom, and regrets. While God's Word is the primary tool for mind transformation, there are some advances being made in other treatments. Sometimes people endure events that traumatize them so destructively that it's like the brain is scarred, and they are never the same. Psychology has labelled this "Post Traumatic Brain Syndrome" or PTSD. When the trauma is so great that the things we have discussed do not resolve it, there may be value in exploring EMDR, Eye Movement Desensitization and Reprocessing. This method does not use cognitive, behavioral, or medication therapy. It activates the brain's own healing mechanism. It is recognized as an effective treatment by the American Psychological Association and other health agencies. For more information, there is a secular book entitled *The Instinct to Heal* written by David Servan-Schreiber, MD, PhD that has valuable information on treating depression, anxiety, and stress without drugs or talk therapy. Using our God-given natural healing process, Dr. Schreiber presents seven approaches, each with proven results, that build on the body's relationship to the brain.

SECOND, MENTAL METAMORPHOSIS ALSO <u>CHANGES HOW YOU SEE YOURSELF</u>.

Deep inside your mind, you have a set of thinking that shapes the way you look at everything including yourself. This self image exists because of experiences and mental thoughts that have shaped you in the past. The simple truth is this: *you always act consistent with this image of yourself.* If you perceive yourself to be worthless, clumsy, and no good, you will act this way. If you perceive yourself to be loved, valued, and God-designed, your behavior will conform to this. The inner world of thoughts shapes your outer world of circumstances. What you display repeatedly on the screen of your working memory will change your outlook and behavior. If you attempt to change behavior without changing your thought life, you are working with second causes—not first causes. This is why biblical meditation is God's way of bringing success to all your endeavors.

THIRD, MENTAL METAMORPHOSIS <u>CHANGES HOW YOU SEE THE WORLD</u>.

Biblical meditation changes your perception of yourself, but it also changes your perception of the world around you. This is your worldview, and it shapes all your reality. With the transformation of your mind, your worldview is radically changed to a biblical worldview. How you look at family life, social justice, business ethics, entertainment, environmental issues, death and life, moral behavior, right and wrong, and virtually every area of life is shaped by your biblical worldview. Seeing things as God sees them means absolute moral truths exist as defined by Scripture. Your mind now processes information through the lens of biblical truth.

THIRD, MENTAL METAMORPHOSIS <u>CHANGES THE WAY YOUR MIND THINKS</u>.

The natural mind is incapable of understanding the things of God. "People who aren't spiritual can't receive these truths from God's Spirit. It all sounds foolish to them and they can't understand it, for only those who are spiritual can understand what the Spirit means" (1 Cor. 2:14 NLT). With the flashlight of the Holy Spirit illuminating your mind, you are given insights into what God has prepared for you. "'No eye has seen, no ear has heard, and no mind has imagined what God has prepared for those who love him.' But it was to us that God revealed these things by his Spirit. For his Spirit searches out everything and shows us God's deep secrets" (1 Cor. 2:9–10 NLT). We sometimes think the "No eye … no ear … no mind has imagined" is what we'll understand when we're in heaven. But notice these things have been revealed now by the Holy Spirit. We have been given the mind of Christ—unique insight and understanding of spiritual things revealed by the Holy Spirit (1 Cor. 2:16). Our mind has a new capacity to think spiritual thoughts because of the indwelling Holy Spirit.

FOURTH, MENTAL METAMORPHOSIS DEFUSES AND SELECTIVELY OVERWRITES BURIED MENTAL IMAGES.

It may help to define the word "defuse." This is different than "diffuse" which means to spread something out. Defuse means to remove the fuse from something that explodes—like a mine or a bomb. It also means to render something harmless. God works to defuse mental tormentors.

What happens to buried anger, jealousies, woundedness, and pornography stored in your long-term memory? You may suffer from deeply scarring memories or traumatic events that it seems you will always remember. A thought can be like a land mine, a buried device that explodes when you walk or drive over it. Someone may get too close to a buried wound and suddenly you have an emotional explosion. As military land mines can be defused through a "render safe procedure" (RSP), mental land mines can also be defused. For example, I can remember many of the events when I've been hurt, but I no longer feel resentment. My emotions don't explode when I recall these events. The Word of God has defused the memory. It is no longer explosive. I am set free.

In the computer world, the only way to permanently erase a file is to overwrite it repeatedly. Hitting DELETE or FORMAT does not permanently remove files—only the visible pathways to the files. Computer files are permanently erased by a process called "disk wiping" or "disk scrubbing"—actually overwriting the unwanted files with new data several times. The government standard (DoD 5220.22-M), considered a medium security level, specifies overwriting a hard drive six times with repetitive numbers.[34]

We've become familiar with terms like malware, viruses, spyware, Trojan horses, and worms that work havoc in our computers. I believe God selectively overwrites the corrupted files in our minds—fears and phobias, scarring put-downs, pornographic images, buried resentments—with forgiveness, joy, patience, courage, gentleness, peace, tenderness, and love. This is the repetitive power of renewing the mind (Rom. 12:2), continually meditating on Scripture as it overwrites the old destructive data.

For example, if your mother screamed at you, "You're a worthless, no good child. You'll never amount to anything," this lie is burned into your mental hard drive. The brain's hard drive doesn't sort out what's true or false. It will be very difficult *not* to act like a worthless, no good person. As a Christian, you begin to read your Bible, and you discover as the Psalmist proclaimed, "You're my place of quiet retreat; I wait for your Word to renew me" (Ps. 119:114 MSG). And one day you read these amazing verses. "Even before he made the world, God loved us and chose us in Christ to be holy and without fault in his eyes. God

---

34. Vangie Beal, "How to Completely Erase a Hard Disk Drive," www.webopedia.com, accessed Sept. 7, 2019.

decided in advance to adopt us into his own family by bringing us to himself through Jesus Christ. This is what he wanted to do, and it gave him great pleasure" (Eph. 1:4–5 NLT).

Wow! God chose me and adopted me into his family, you think to yourself. As you continue to read and meditate, the Word of God is repeatedly overwriting that old "you're a worthless, no-good person, who will never amount to anything" file. Your view of yourself changes. You begin to carry yourself differently. You're a child of God adopted into an eternal family. You're the apple of God's eye (Ps. 17:8). As you meditate on Scripture, you are overwriting the damaging lie your mother planted in your mind. You will likely always remember what your mother told you, but the false data is written over with new transforming information.

Here's another illustration of what takes place. Before you became a Christian, when certain things went wrong, you may have cut loose with a rapid-fire string of profanity. It was like a trigger on a pistol that unleashed a bullet barrage of cursing and swearing. This nearly automatic response was rooted in your memory bank. Once you become a believer, the Holy Spirit convicts you about the filth that comes out of your mouth when you're upset. You begin to meditate on Scriptures that remind you to not let any unwholesome word proceed from your mouth (Eph. 4:29). The Word begins to overwrite the trigger response and the day comes when an event occurs that makes you very angry. In the past, this would have triggered a string of profanity, but now you no longer swear as you once did. This is "metamorphosis of the mind."

The brain-computer comparisons may help us understand our minds in some measure, but in the final analysis, the analogy falls short of grasping the complexity of the human mind. As God's Word penetrates into our minds and mental strongholds are taken captive, buried negative thoughts and feelings are defused, written over, and selectively erased; the destructive fangs are removed, and their controlling influence is rendered null and void. God's Word overpowers these potentially destructive thoughts.

GO AHEAD AND CHANGE YOUR MIND

It's your right to "change your mind." No one can stop you. So what's holding you back? Start reading and meditating on God's Word every day. Discover the "winning edge" for a new way of living.

Biblical meditation gives you *an edge* to win, to be successful in your endeavors. As David said, "Your commands give me an edge on my enemies; they never become obsolete" (Ps. 119:98 MSG). Your mind is a powerhouse of potential. Unleash God's power to transform your neck-top computer that controls your every impulse, behavior, decision, feeling, action, or reaction. And remember, *since your mind controls your behavior, let God control your mind and your behavior will change.* Power in weakness is mental torment turned to quiet trust—God's perfect peace for you when your thoughts are fixed on him (Is. 26:3). Go ahead and change your mind. You have nothing to lose and everything to gain.

Or to put it more simply, to quote some unknown poet,

> Your mind is a garden,
> Your thoughts are seeds.
> You can grow flowers, or
> Just grow weeds.

So what's growing in your garden?

DAY FIVE—CHAPTER THREE

TIME OUT

Power Thoughts for Your Time Alone With God

The Word of God defuses buried negative thoughts and feelings rendering them null and void—the destructive fangs are removed.

◊ Read Philippians 4:4–8 in your Bible and then compare it with this paraphrase.

Delight yourselves in God, yes, find your joy in him at all times. Have a reputation for gentleness, and never forget the nearness of your Lord.

Don't worry over anything whatever; tell God every detail of your needs in earnest and thankful prayer, and the peace of God which transcends human understanding, will keep constant guard over your hearts and minds as they rest in Christ Jesus.

Here is a last piece of advice. If you believe in goodness and if you value the approval of God, fix your minds on the things which are holy and right and pure and beautiful and good. Model your conduct on what you have learned from me, on what I have told you and shown you, and you will find the God of peace will be with you. (Phil. 4:4–8 PHI. NT)

◊ What is your "game plan" to guard your mind? What are your personal standards? Write out your plan. Use a separate sheet of paper if necessary.

TIME TOGETHER

SESSION THREE

DEFUSING TORMENTORS IN THE MIND

Your mind is a powerhouse of potential, one of the most complex objects in the known universe. The component parts are staggering: one hundred billion nerve cells connecting with each other up to 60,000 times through 100,000 miles of nerve fibers—all of this going on between your ears. Wise Solomon said it this way, "Be careful what you think because your thoughts run your life" (Prov. 4:23 NCV). Since your mind controls your behavior, let God control your mind, and your behavior will change. Now is the time to let God take control of your mind. It's your right to "change your mind," so let's do it.

CONNECT

◊ Choose one of the following as your opener:

1. Tell about a time when a smell, taste, sound, or sight triggered a warm memory—or an unpleasant memory.

2. In junior high, high school, or college, what pressure did you feel to fit in and conform to the crowd? How is it different or similar now?

GROW

◊ Discuss the drawing of the mind that follows. Pause after each part of the drawing and discuss it. Identify examples of how a violent TV program or an off-color story you hear at work gets stuck in your memory.

Input

or the word of God is alive and
)owerful. It is sharper than the
arpest two-edged sword, cutting
veen soul and spirit, between joint
marrow. It exposes our innermost
)ughts and desires. (Heb. 4:12 NLT)

Output

Do not be conformed to this world, but
be transformed by the renewing of
your mind. (Rom. 12:2 NASB)
You will keep in perfect peace all who
trust in you, all whose thoughts are
fixed on you! (Is. 26:3 NLT)

WORKING MEMORY
Computer Screen

Fix your thoughts on what is true, and honorable, and right, and pure, and
lovely, and admirable. Think about things that are excellent and worthy of
praise. (Phil. 4:8 NLT)

SHORT-TERM MEMORY
Random Access Memory

I have hidden your word in my heart that I might not sin against you. (Ps. 119:11 NIV)

LONG-TERM MEMORY
Hard Drive Memory

Take captive every thought to make it obedient to Christ. (2 Cor. 10:5 NIV)

Jealousies   Hatred   Pornographic Images   Fetishes

Cynical Thinking   Resentments   Rage   Abuse

Controlling Fears   Gloom   Regrets

Changing Your Mind

© 2015, Dave Beckwith

◊ Read Philippians 4:4–9 phrase by phrase, pausing to unwrap each key thought.

> Always be full of joy in the Lord. I say it again—rejoice! Let everyone see that you are considerate in all you do. Remember, the Lord is coming soon.
>
> Don't worry about anything; instead, pray about everything. Tell God what you need, and thank him for all he has done. Then you will experience God's peace, which exceeds anything we can understand. His peace will guard your hearts and minds as you live in Christ Jesus.
>
> And now, dear brothers and sisters, one final thing. Fix your thoughts on what is true, and honorable, and right, and pure, and lovely, and admirable. Think about things that are excellent and worthy of praise. Keep putting into practice all you learned and received from me—everything you heard from me and saw me doing. Then the God of peace will be with you. (Phil. 4:4–9 NLT)

◊ For vivid contrast, as a group, select an opposite value to insert in verse 8 to replace each positive value. The first opposite is supplied to show how this works.

> Whatever is false (the opposite of true), whatever is _____ (noble), whatever is _____ (right), whatever is _____ (pure), whatever is _____ (lovely), whatever is _____ (admirable)—if anything is _____ (excellent) or _____ (praiseworthy)—think about such things.

◊ When finished, read it out loud with the negative words inserted. How similar is this to the culture around you?

◊ Optional: discuss these questions as time permits.

1. Why do you think God didn't erase the hard drive of our brains to remove destructive thoughts and memories when we accepted Christ?

2. Have you found this to be true? "Your commands give me an edge on my enemies; they never become obsolete" (Ps. 119:98 MSG). In what ways?

3. What is your worldview? Is it a biblical worldview?

4. Discuss the best way to guide and protect children in choices regarding television, internet, movies, and video games?

◊ Read aloud in unison the "Changing My Mind" verse for this week.

A Mental Makeover
Don't copy the
behavior and customs
of this world, but let
God transform you
into a new person by
changing the way you
think.
—Rom. 12:2 NLT

APPLY

◊ What are the negative mental influences (TV, movies, reading, work environment, etc.) you face each week?

143

◊ As a group, read and discuss these benefits of biblical meditation.

Biblical Meditation ...

... isn't emptying your mind; it's filling your mind with God.

... doesn't require isolation; it fits with the flow of your busy life.

... doesn't complicate your life; it's your compass in the midst of chaos.

... overcomes intimidation with God-courage (Josh. 1:6–9).

... builds strong faith (Rom. 10:17).

... will help you overcome temptation (Ps. 119:11).

... is God's prescription to heal your mind and emotions (Rom. 12:1–2).

... is an effective antidote to worry (Phil. 4:6–8).

... changes your attitude and outlook on life (Phil. 4:7).

... brings success to your endeavors (Ps. 1:2–3).

... is the key to perfect peace (Isa. 26:3).

◊ What is your "game plan" for practicing meditation? Share it with the group.

PRAY

◊ Spend time praying for each other with brief sentence prayers. Close by praying this prayer out loud in unison. "May the words of my mouth and the meditation of my heart be pleasing to you, O LORD, my rock and my redeemer" (Ps. 19:14 NLT).

SHARE

◊ Look for an opportunity to start a conversation this week. Here are some questions that may start a dialogue:

1. Do you think the human mind can be changed?

2. What weighs heavily on your mind about our world today?

3. How do you handle anxiety and stress?

◊ Let this be your prayer as you ask God to lead you to someone to share your faith with. "… always *being* ready to make a defense to everyone who asks you to give an account for the hope that is in you, yet with gentleness and reverence;" (1 Pet. 3:15).

CHAPTER FOUR

RELEASING RESENTMENTS

Resentment is like drinking poison and waiting
or the other person to die.
—Saint Augustine

We were excited to have guests joining us for lunch at our home for a Good Friday celebration. All the preparations had been made, and the food was on the table. Just before I led in prayer, Joanne took a phone call in the office and motioned for the group to go ahead and eat. About thirty minutes later, she returned to the table with tears running down her cheeks. Her tears created an awkward moment for the guests and us as well. Sensing her pain and embarrassment, I put my arm around her and asked, "Who was that on the phone? What happened?" Through her tears, she attempted to explain that one of the leading women of the church had verbally ripped into her.

Easter Sunday had been planned as a big community outreach, and Joanne, as administrative secretary for the church where I served as pastor, had attempted to shore up an area that had been overlooked. This woman and her husband felt Joanne's well-intended efforts were meddling in their area. Joanne quickly apologized hoping to put the matter to rest, but for some reason, it remained unresolved. This woman's words hurt deeply, and her unwillingness to accept Joanne's apology hurt even worse.

The Easter services were packed with record attendance and many decisions for Christ, but the joy we felt was clouded by what had happened. Usually, the misunderstanding would have been quickly resolved and forgotten; instead, it festered and escalated into a bitter distrust of our leadership. As the conflict continued to intensify, Joanne drove her car to a quiet spot and sobbed. Crying out to God, she asked, "Why?" It didn't make sense. She'd done nothing with ill will. Her efforts were intended to help a ministry, and now she was being maligned for her hard work.

The couple had been at the church for many years and had a significant power base. They wanted an austere atmosphere in the services, and they felt everyone should enter the sanctuary and sit in silence before the service began. During the service, any outburst of laughter or spontaneous applause was, in their way of thinking, disgraceful. However, we encouraged warm interaction, humor, and spontaneous clapping when appropriate. These differences set in motion an intense struggle, all of it fueled by the unresolved issue. Each month, the couple attended the board meeting to present their concerns about the church, including a list of what I was doing wrong as senior pastor. I protested to the board this was wrong and hurtful to me, but they said, "We have to let people have their say." I grew to dread going to board meetings.

Though the ministry continued to grow, our lives were in pain. Bitterness began to weaken our effectiveness. The joy of ministry was drained and attempts at reconciliation were unsuccessful, even with the assistance of a veteran pastor. Bitter resentment took root in our lives like a crop of weeds in a beautiful garden. But God was at work in our lives. (You'll read about the miraculous ending to this story later in the chapter.)

RESENTMENT FUEL

Is life fair? If I had a dollar for every time I heard my two daughters protest, "It's not fair," I'd have a good start on a retirement fund. Perhaps it would have been simpler to shorten, "It's not fair" to "INF," as in, "I did the dishes last night. INF." "She always gets to stay up late. INF." Joanne and I went to great lengths to equalize everything. How naïve! After several years of INF-negotiating, I finally wised up and said, "You're right. Life isn't fair. Deal with it."

My daughters were more right than they realized: life is not fair. Not every wrong will be made right, nor every injustice made equitable in this life. Many things simply aren't fair. Life comes packaged with plenty of "INF" stuff—resentment fuel. Who hasn't experienced one or more of these potential causes for resentment?

◊ An antagonist makes your life miserable

◊ A promotion you deserved goes to someone else

◊ Someone you thought was a friend stabs you in the back

◊ An unscrupulous salesman talks you into an unwise purchase

◊ Your marriage partner is unfaithful

◊ A fabricated rumor circulates that damages your reputation

◊ You do the work, but someone else gets the credit

◊ You are maligned for taking a courageous stand for truth and justice

◊ Your grown child no longer speaks with you

◊ You are lied to

◊ You work tirelessly at your job but get fired

◊ A confidence is violated

◊ You suffer a permanent injury from a driver who ran a red light

◊ You attempt to help someone, and they turn against you

◊ Money you're owed remains unpaid

◊ A broken promise leaves you disappointed

THE ROOTS OF RESENTMENTS

During their wilderness wandering, the Israelites came face to face with adversity that fueled resentment.

> Soon the people began to complain about their hardship, and the LORD heard everything they said. Then the LORD's anger blazed against them, and he sent a fire to rage among them, and he destroyed some of the people in the outskirts of the camp. Then the people screamed to Moses for help, and when he prayed to the LORD, the fire stopped. After that, the area was known as Taberah (which means "the place of burning"), because fire from the LORD had burned among them there.

> Then the foreign rabble who were traveling with the Israelites began to crave the good things of Egypt. And the people of Israel

also began to complain. "Oh, for some meat!" they exclaimed. "We remember the fish we used to eat for free in Egypt. And we had all the cucumbers, melons, leeks, onions, and garlic we wanted. But now our appetites are gone. All we ever see is this manna!" (Num. 11:1-6 NLT)

Resentment invaded the camp and gripped the people's attitudes. The people complained about their hardships, and resentment spread like flu in the pew. God's displeasure with their attitude was evident as fire from the LORD burned among them. The phrase is used in 1 Kings 18:38 to describe fire ignited by lightning. Whether it was lightning-caused or not, the fire that burned among them was disciplinary action from God. Despite the fire from God, their discontent still smoldered: "If only we had meat to eat!" they cried. Moses, discouraged by their bellyaching, went before God. "Where am I supposed to get meat for all these people? They keep whining to me, saying, 'Give us meat to eat!' I can't carry all these people by myself! The load is far too heavy! If this is how you intend to treat me, just go ahead and kill me. Do me a favor and spare me this misery!" (Num. 11:13-15 NLT).

In my opinion, Moses was the second greatest leader of all time—Jesus being number one. My friend, Ken Poure who led Hume Lake Christian Conference Center for decades, said, "Moses was the greatest camp director of all time—two to three million campers and no facilities." This great leader is having a major melt down. Moses isn't an immature believer. He met with God on Mt. Sinai. He's a tough veteran of the faith. With all this, resentment still got a stranglehold on him. He complained that the burden was too heavy, and he submitted his resignation. His despondency was so deep, he asked God to take his life. Moses isn't suicidal, but he is one step from it.

Resentments will take you down—just as it did for Moses. It doesn't matter how mature you are or committed to the Lord, resentments can set up camp in your life and drain your joy. When you're wrestling with a bitter resentment, you will soon become aware of how insidiously powerful the resentment is. You may try to suppress the thought or pretend it doesn't exist— and then it grips you again. You mumble to yourself, *Why does this scoundrel get away with what he did? Why did this happen to me?* The truth is this: *you and I are powerless to release our resentments.*

This is where we need "power in weakness." In our struggle, we acknowledge our powerlessness and ask God to release us from resentment by his power. It is a moment of surrender … the beginning of repeated surrenders. This will be developed further in the four steps at the end of this chapter. To better understand resentments, there are four types of root issues that feed this issue.

Type One: Resentment regarding life circumstances

You may feel that circumstances always bounce the wrong way for you. Questions similar to these may float in your mind:

◊ How did I end up with a job I dislike?

◊ Why is it always my car that breaks down?

◊ I've been honest and hardworking, but I still can't pay my bills each month.

◊ Why am I sidelined with pain and poor health while my friends are active and healthy?

Adversity, hardship, and wilderness-wandering were the initial resentments that gripped the Israelites, and God was clearly displeased when they complained about their hardships (Num. 11:1). Elsewhere in the Bible, God warns against a complaining attitude. James says, "Don't grumble about each other, brothers and sisters, or you will be judged. For look—the Judge is standing at the door!" (James 5:9 NLT). Even though the Judge at the door refers to the Lord's return, I can't read this verse without imagining Jesus standing in the doorway of the room listening if I grumble.

All of us experience days when we don't feel well—not enough sleep, a headache, allergies, flu-like symptoms. Since it's wrong to complain, does this mean you should pretend you're okay while your grumpy attitude tells everyone you're not? No. Instead, it's important to report what you're going through rather than faking it. Simply say, "I'm not feeling well today, and I could use some extra grace."

On the other hand, if someone continuously whines and moans about every ache and pain, people will find it depressing to be around them. Paul warned, "Do all things without grumbling or disputing." Then he explains why this is so important: "… so that you will prove yourselves to be blameless and innocent, children of God above reproach in the midst of a crooked and perverse generation, among whom you appear as lights in the world," (Phil. 2:14-15). If you're known for constant complaining about work conditions, the weather, how unfair everyone is to you, the light of your Christian witness goes out. A complaining Christian is a contradiction; grumbling negates an effective witness to a lost world. A church with a lot of whining, complaining, and nitpicking will be highly ineffective at reaching people for Christ.

What's the difference between *complaining* and *explaining*? This is the key distinction. Complaining drips with resentment; at the core, it's a bitter, unthankful attitude, ultimately toward God. *Explaining* an adversity is done with a grateful and joyful attitude. It's either "griping" or "gladness," "grumbling" or "gratefulness" in your attitude.

DAY ONE—CHAPTER FOUR

TIME OUT

Power Thoughts for Your Time Alone With God

Complaining drips with resentment; at the core, it's a bitter, unthankful attitude toward God.

◊ What things are you are most likely to complain about? Did you grumble about something this week?

◊ Read James 5:7-18. Make some notes on what the passage says to do in various situations.

1. When you're suffering, be _____ like the farmer.

2. Don't _____ against each other, or you will be judged.

3. Don't _____ by heaven or earth or by anything else.

4. When you're in trouble, _____.

5. When you're happy, _____ _____.

6. When you're sick, _____ _____.

7. When you sin, confess your sins to _____ _____.

◊ How will you apply this passage the next time you find reasons to complain?

◊ Let's consider a day when you didn't get enough sleep and feel achy all over. How would you express this to those around you without displaying an unthankful attitude toward God?

◊ Go to the back of your book for this week's meditation verse titled "Weed Killer for a Bitter Root." Carry it with you or put it someplace where you can direct your thoughts to it throughout the day and memorize it.

TYPE TWO: RESENTMENT AGAINST PEOPLE WHO HAVE HURT OR DISAPPOINTED YOU

We all have experienced hurt and pain from other people, and this type of resentment is usually deeper and more difficult to uproot. This may include being hurt by your parents or your children. Friends (or former friends) may have done things that brought deep pain into your life. They embarrassed you, made a caustic remark, betrayed you, put you down, and you live with the memory. The pain is deep and intensely personal.

An authority figure, such as an employer, school teacher, church leader, or law enforcement officer, may be a source of bitterness. One of my close friends was deeply hurt by a school teacher/coach who treated the athletes with special favors but ridiculed and picked on anyone who wasn't a jock. Another friend was falsely accused by his boss of stealing from the company. Even though he was exonerated of the charges, and it came to light that the boss lied because he felt threatened by the employee, this accusation ruined my friend's career in that field. In Numbers 11, Israel's complaints regarding adversity (Resentment Type One) also included resentment directed against Moses, the authority figure (Resentment Type Two).

Have you experienced the loss of a once close friend? Did a trusted friend turn against you? David had such an experience. "It is not an enemy who taunts me— I could bear that. It is not my foes who so arrogantly insult me— I could have hidden from them. Instead, it is you—my equal, my companion and close friend. What good fellowship we once enjoyed as we walked together to the house of God" (Ps. 55:12-14 NLT). This person was a former confidant, companion, and a close friend. David and this former friend worshiped God together. What went wrong in the relationship? We don't know the details, but David states this: "As for my companion, he betrayed his friends; he broke his promises. His words are as smooth as butter, but in his heart is war. His words are as soothing as lotion, but underneath are daggers!" (Ps. 55:20-21 NLT). This former friend was a back-stabbing betrayer. The pain ran deep. When your companion— someone who was once your close friend—betrays you and stabs you in the back, remember Jesus felt the pain of Judas, the one who delivered him over to death.

If you've experienced this kind of loss, the closeness you once enjoyed in your relationship makes the loss sting even more. It's helpful to process this by writing a letter you never send. Describe what the person did and your feelings about it. You may want to read the letter to someone you can confide in and allow that person to help you process your feelings. Then tear up what you wrote. In some cases, you may want to write another letter that would be appropriate to send, explaining your sense of loss and seeking reconciliation.

TYPE THREE: RESENTMENT AGAINST YOURSELF

You may resent senseless things you've done, your lack of resolve and will-power, or a foolish decision that brought great pain in your life. You may ask yourself questions similar to these:

◊ Why do I yell at my kids?

◊ Why didn't I take better care of my body?

◊ Why did I foolishly blow all that money?

◊ Why do I always open my mouth when I know I should keep quiet?

Paul's agony in Romans 7 is a self-directed type-three resentment: "What I am doing, I do not understand; for I am not practicing what I *would* like to *do*, but I am doing the very thing I hate" (Rom. 7:15). Resentment against yourself and resentment of God are very similar; however, the cause of your self-resentment is usually something you had some degree of control over—your will was involved. The fourth type, God-resentment, which follows, is something you did not have control over.

TYPE FOUR: RESENTMENT AGAINST GOD

Do you have questions similar to these?

◊ Why am I afflicted with a debilitating disease while my godless neighbor enjoys robust health and great prosperity?

◊ Why did God make my nose crooked?

◊ Why was I born into a dysfunctional home?

◊ Why am I so average—nothing noteworthy to help me get ahead?

The other three types of resentments—circumstances, people who wronged you, and yourself—often reflect this fourth underlying resentment, the granddaddy of them all: resentment *against God.* After all, "The LORD makes some poor and others rich; he brings some down and lifts others up" (1 Sam. 2:7 NLT). Many reject God or resist his control over their lives because deep down they feel God has given them a raw deal. Isaiah warns, "What sorrow awaits those who argue with their Creator? Does a clay pot argue with its maker? Does the clay dispute with the one who shapes it, saying, "'Stop, you're doing it wrong!'" (Isa. 45:9 NLT). God takes responsibility for shaping you.

Each type of resentment often includes one or more of the other types. Moses got hit with all four types of resentments in this singular incident. Take another look at Numbers 11:13-15 in this paraphrase. Here we see that resentment simmering under the surface makes it difficult to trust God.

He prayed:

> I am your servant, LORD, so why are you doing this to me? What have I done to deserve this? You've made me responsible for all these people, but they're not my children. You told me to nurse them along and to carry them to the land you promised their ancestors. They keep whining for meat, but where can I get meat for them? This job is too much for me. How can I take care of all these people by myself? If this is the way you're going to treat me, just kill me now and end my miserable life! (Num. 11:11-15 CEV)

While this is primarily a God-resentment, you will notice Moses had all four types of resentments.

1. Resentment of circumstances: "Where can I get meat for them?"

2. Resentment of others: "They keep whining for meat."

3. Resentment of self: "This job is too much for me."

4. Resentment of God: "If this is the way you're going to treat me, just kill me now and end my miserable life!"

DAY TWO—CHAPTER FOUR

TIME OUT

Power Thoughts for Your Time Alone With God

You meant evil against me, but God meant it for good.
—Gen. 50:20

◊ Read Genesis 37:19-36 and 50:18-20.

◊ Using the worksheet in Appendix C or a blank sheet of paper, do a personal inventory, including unfair circumstances, mistreatment by others, disappointments regarding yourself, or resentful feelings toward God. Make certain your list remains private. We will work with this inventory later in the chapter.

◊ Put a 1, 2, 3, or 4 next to each resentment on your list to identify the type of resentment (resentments are often more than one type):
Type 1: Resentment of circumstances
Type 2: Resentment of others
Type 3: Resentment of yourself
Type 4: Resentment of God

◊ During your time of prayer, ask God to give you a Joseph perspective ("You meant evil against me, but God meant it for good") regarding those who've hurt you.

THE CAUSTIC EFFECTS OF RESENTMENTS

Resentments work like a slow-acting poison, eating away at physical, mental, emotional, and spiritual health. When someone says, "If it's the last thing I do, I'll get even with that slime-ball," it may truly be the last thing they do. Many have dropped dead from a heart attack while brimming with resentment. A scoundrel of a guy named Nabal, whom the Bible describes as surly and mean, mistreated David and his men and then spent the night getting drunk. In the morning, he suffered a massive heart attack or stroke. Nabal's heart failed him, and he became like stone. His body was paralyzed, and he died ten days later (1 Sam. 25:37-38).

Resentments need a bold label that says, WARNING: TOXIC POISON. When David was filled with resentments and regrets, he said, "I'm on the edge of losing it—the pain in my gut keeps burning" (Ps. 38:17 MSG). These insidious thoughts attach to your mind and emotions, and they are "re-sent" (root of the word resentment)—played over-and-over again. This process of ruminating over resentments pollutes and poisons your inner being. "Watch out that no poisonous root of bitterness grows up to trouble you, corrupting many" (Heb. 12:15 NLT). The poison of resentment will inevitably seep from your life into the lives of others—your spouse, your children, your employees, your friends. Proverbs warns, "The fool who provokes his family to anger and resentment will finally have nothing worthwhile left. He shall be the servant of a wiser man" (Prov. 11:29 TLB).

The word "bitterness" is the Greek word *pikria*, which means "to cut, to prick." A bitter person often makes caustic, cutting comments. The Psalmist said regarding his bitter enemies, "Listen to the filth that comes from their mouths; their words cut like swords" (Ps. 59:7 NLT). I picture little, flashing daggers popping out when they speak. Rabbi Yehuda Berg stated, "Hurt people hurt people.

That's how pain patterns get passed on, generation after generation after generation."[35] It's also true that hurt people hurt themselves. In a strange irony, when you resent someone, you may actually begin to resemble their behaviors and attitudes. Many with bitter resentment toward a parent have said, "I'll never be like my mom or dad." Ten years later, they're horrified to see their resemblance to the parent they despise. The caustic effects of resentment are 24/7—always with you unless released and healed. Medical doctor S. I. McMillen wrote, "The moment I start hating a man, I become his slave. I can't enjoy my work anymore because he even controls my thoughts. My resentments produce too many stress hormones in my body and I become fatigued after only a few hours of work. The work I formerly enjoyed is now drudgery. Even vacations cease to give me pleasure. ... The man I hate hounds me wherever I go. I can't escape his tyrannical grasp on my mind."[36]

While speaking at a camp for a week, I noticed a man about thirty years of age in the audience, listening very intently but with a noticeable and somewhat obnoxious facial twitch. The twitch was so pronounced I found it distracting while I spoke. After the session, he asked if he could speak with me. We sat down in the front of the chapel and talked until after midnight. His life was full of deep bitterness about his ex-wife and an employer who let him go. I was feeling quite hopeless to assist him with all the brimming anger. Finally, about one a.m., I suggested we kneel together by a bench in the chapel and pray. He began to sob deeply as he asked God for forgiveness and to take away his resentment of his ex-wife and former employer.

When we stood up, I put an arm on his shoulder, and I noticed the facial twitch had stopped. I didn't think too much

35. Rabbi Yehuda Berg, "Motivational Quotes," http://www.motivationalquotesabout.com/from/yehuda-berg, accessed Sept. 7, 2019.
36. S. I. McMillen, M.D., *None of These Diseases* (Old Tappen, New Jersey: Fleming H. Revell Co., 1967), 72.

about it, but the next morning at breakfast, I again noticed the absence of the twitch. Throughout the remainder of the week, the entire camp was astounded at the change in his appearance, the absence of the facial twitch, the smile on his face, and the change in his attitude. A year later, I spoke in the area again and asked about him. He was traveling, so I didn't get to see him, but the pastor assured me he was doing well, and the facial twitch had not returned. The twitch was likely related to *Tourette* syndrome, a condition characterized by eye-blinking, coughing, throat clearing, sniffing, and facial movements; causes include a variety of genetic and environmental factors. It would be erroneous to assume all cases of Tourette syndrome are caused by unresolved emotional issues. However, in this case, the pent-up bitterness and resentment were clearly the cause of the facial twitch.

Resentments are like the mercury in a thermometer, rising and then subsiding, depending on the heat and pressure in life. The resentment in the thermometer is toxic to the human system, a poison that can easily leak out and infect others. The only way to deal effectively with resentment is to drain the mercury from the thermometer. When this occurs, the outcome is the wonderful freedom of resentment-free living.

DAY THREE—CHAPTER FOUR

TIME OUT
Power Thoughts for Your Time Alone With God

Resentments work like a slow-acting poison eating away at physical, mental, emotional, and spiritual health.

◊ Think of a time when you were upset and resentful. How did this resentment affect your physical, mental, emotional, and spiritual health? How was your sleep affected?

◊ Read Hebrews 12:1-3, 14-15. Observation: your mind can be "fixed on Jesus" (vs. 2) or "fixed on an all-consuming resentment" (vs. 15). In your experience, how does one affect the other?

◊ Look again at Hebrews 12:1. To change the focus of your mind to Jesus rather than your resentment, make this your prayer today.

> Lord, help me throw off everything that hinders and holds me back (my anger and resentments, feelings of failure and shame) and any sin that is currently entangling me and pulling me down. I am willing—set me free. Give me the strength to run with perseverance the race you have for me. Change my mental focus and allow me to fix my eyes on you, Jesus.

BREAKING A RESENTMENT HEADLOCK

If you're expecting every wrong to be made right and every injustice to be made equitable in this life, you're in for a life of disappointment. Many things aren't fair and never will be in this lifetime. Everyone I know has suffered enough injustices and wrongs to remain bitter for their entire life. They could crawl into a corner in a fetal position and feel sorry for themselves all their days. A choice must be made: release resentments or remain mentally, emotionally, and spiritually crippled. The sidelines of the game of life are lined with once effective, multi-talented, bitter people, now crippled with arthritic-like resentments.

Having personally wrestled with my own resentments and having worked with those gripped by them, I am convinced resentments are one of Satan's primary strongholds to choke the spiritual life of a believer.

Here are four crucial steps—steps you will use over-and-over again—to uproot resentments and be set free.

STEP ONE: I AM POWERLESS TO RELEASE MY RESENTMENTS.

Most people attempt to deal with resentments in one of two ways, neither of which work. One method is to bury the resentful feelings by telling yourself, *I'll ignore the pain, and it will go away sooner or later.* The other approach is to deny the hurt—put on your superman or superwoman cape, pretend to be invincible, and tell yourself, *I'm tough. They tried to hurt me, but there's no way they can get to me, and I'm not going to give them the satisfaction of thinking they can.* You may appear strong and confident, but you're simply suppressing the pain. Buried, unhealed resentments have long-term effects: broken relationships, distrust of others, a sour attitude, inability to be close, illicit sexual escapades, risk-taking, or a variety of pain-numbing behaviors like overeating, alcohol abuse, drug use, etc.

James 3:14 says, "If you are bitterly jealous and there is selfish ambition in your heart, don't cover up the truth with boasting and lying" (NLT). Harboring bitter envy is carrying around a "boat load" of ugly feelings that are anchored in your soul. James goes on to identify the two ways mentioned above that most people use to deal with bitterness. One is to bury the resentment and pretend it doesn't exist—*covering up the truth.* The other is to assume arrogantly it's no big deal, and you can handle it on your own—*boasting about it.*

Hopefully, no one has ever put a headlock on you (unless you're a competitive wrestler). This is a method of attacking and restraining someone by putting an arm around their head, usually at the neck. This method can cause death by asphyxiation if held long enough. Deep-rooted resentments are like a "spiritual headlock," exerting overwhelming control. You're in the grip, the stranglehold of something bigger and more powerful than you. To break the stranglehold and regain your edge, you must appropriate God's power. The first step to being set free begins with a prayer of surrender, a cry for help: "Lord Jesus, I'm powerless to break the stranglehold of my resentments."

STEP TWO: I'M WILLING FOR JESUS CHRIST TO SET ME FREE FROM MY RESENTMENTS.

The key word is "willing." You've likely met people controlled by anger and resentments, but they don't want to let go. What will they have to talk about? They enjoy retelling the sordid details of all the times they've been wronged to anyone who will listen. They begin to display their resentments—how they carry themselves, their general demeanor, even the lines in their face. Their resentments become their identity.

Being "willing to release" a resentment is quite different from the "ability to release" a resentment, as I've discovered in counseling those with a deep-seated bitterness. I listen to them spill their story of someone who's hurt them deeply, and then they say, "I don't know if I'll ever be able to forgive this person. Every time I see them, the pain resurfaces. I've tried to forgive them, but I just can't let go of the hurt. I can't forgive them." First, I respond by agreeing with them. "You're right. You can't forgive them. This is something beyond your ability, but don't despair. This is exactly where God wants you to be." Then I explain further. "I'm not asking if you're able to forgive them. I'm asking you if you're willing to forgive them." Finally they say, "Okay. I'm willing." This is the beginning of a breakthrough. Willingness is the second step—and a mandatory one—to be set free.

STEP THREE: I CHOOSE TO ALLOW GOD TO RIGHT THIS WRONG IN HIS TIME.

Resentments are often rooted in some injustice. Something inside you screams for the wrong to be made right. Like a balance and a scale, a wrong tips the scale of justice, creating a driving need to balance the scale. This is why revenge, though wrong and destructive, seems so inviting.

When hurt, it's normal to want the wrong made right. Why? Justice needs to be done and the equilibrium of fairness restored.

You may fear that the one who hurt you will get off without consequences. Letting go seems the most unnatural thing to do.

Most Bible scholars believe that as Paul wrote 2 Timothy, he was in the cold and filth of the Mamertine Prison in Rome, awaiting possible execution. I'll never forget the experience of visiting this prison, one of the oldest jails in the world, dating back some 2,500 years. The jail is constructed with an upper and lower level. Condemned prisoners were thrown into the circular lower room through a hole in the center of the upper-level floor. The lower section is solid granite, round and approximately thirteen feet in diameter and six and a half feet high. It has little light and air from the outside, and no sanitation. An iron door opens to a passageway that leads to the Tiber River. Many of the prisoners died from filth and disease while others died from strangulation or starvation. To dispose of a body, guards opened the iron door and dumped it into the passageway that emptied into the river.[37]

In the darkness of this filthy hole, Paul wrote his "swan song," the last words we have from this great apostle. We don't know if he was executed or if he was released and later traveled to Spain. What we do know is that he expected to be put to death. In the fourth chapter of 2 Timothy, Paul remembered those who deserted him, and in particular that no one supported him when he was on trial. Paul's heart of forgiveness is evident when he says, "May it not be counted against them" (4:16). He also remembered the injuries inflicted on him by a man named Alexander, and though he didn't mention the offense, Paul was deeply hurt. "Alexander, the metalworker, has hurt me in many ways. But the Lord will pay him back for what he has done" (2 Tim. 4:14 CEV).

---

37. John Parker, Tour of Bible Lands, May 7, 1975.

Paul responded in two ways, both very important. *First, he acknowledged the personal injury.* Paul didn't try to play tough by pretending it was no big deal. It hurt, and he admitted to being wounded. This is crucial to effectively process a resentment. *Second, he assigned to God the responsibility for making it right.* He put this on "God's To-do List" by saying, "The Lord will pay him back for what he has done." In 1 Timothy 1:20, Paul mentions an Alexander, who was disciplined and turned over to Satan. This may be the same person though we can't be certain of this.

On occasion, revenge has raced through my mind, and though I knew it was wrong, it was enticing. With God's prompting, rather than responding with revenge, I did what Paul did, inserting the name of the person in the verse and asking the Lord to repay:

"_____ has hurt me in many ways.

The Lord will pay them back for what they have done."

When I've surrendered a point of resentment, I've sometimes seen God bring astounding repayment into the person's life within a relatively short period of time. To our surprise, one couple who'd hurt us came to apologize. God allowed them to experience precisely what they did to us, and through this, they realized the pain they'd caused. In other situations, I know God is at work making things right though it isn't evident to me how he's doing it. Bottom line: *put the repayment of a wrong done to you on "God's To-do List" and leave it there.*

STEP FOUR: I YIELD MY RESENTMENTS TO CHRIST AND CHOOSE TO FORGIVE THOSE WHO'VE WRONGED ME.

Feel the pain, acknowledge the hurt, and ask Christ to heal the deepest resentment in your heart. As you pray, allow him to bring to mind your own weaknesses and failures. Confess your sins and the pain you've brought to others, as you receive Christ's healing for the pain inflicted by others. Visualize yourself there with Christ on the cross, identified in his suffering: "He personally carried our sins in his body on the cross so that we can be dead to sin and live for what is right. By his wounds you are healed" (1 Pet. 2:24 NLT). In the nail-scarred hands of Christ, we find healing.

Forgiveness is primarily a choice of your will rather than a feeling. From a human standpoint, forgiveness is extremely difficult if not impossible. The power to forgive comes from Christ's forgiveness of your sins. Forgiveness is not forgetting the incidents—it's releasing those involved. Forgiving and being forgiven are inseparable. "If you forgive those who sin against you, your heavenly Father will forgive you. But if you refuse to forgive others, your Father will not forgive your sins" (Mt. 6:14-15 NLT). Forgiveness doesn't wait for others to acknowledge their wrong and apologize, as they may never own up to the hurt they caused. When you forgive, *you're* the one set free.

DAY FOUR—CHAPTER FOUR
TIME OUT

Power Thoughts for Your Time Alone With God

Forgiveness is primarily a choice of your will rather than a feeling.

◊ Read Ephesians 4:25-32.

◊ Pray through each of the four steps to release the resentments you wrote down on Day Two.

Apply Step One: I'm powerless to release my resentments. Pray through the resentments on your list, recognizing you are powerless to deal with these yourself. Ask him to break the "mental headlock."

Apply Step Two: I'm willing for Jesus Christ to set me free from my resentments. Go over each resentment on your list and pray, "Lord, I'm willing to release this resentment." Put a "W" next to each resentment to indicate this moment of willingness and surrender.

Apply Step Three: I choose to allow God to right this wrong in his time. Paul was deeply hurt when he wrote, "Alexander, the metalworker, has hurt me in many ways. But the Lord will pay him back for what he has done" (2 Tim. 4:14 CEV). Take the two steps Paul did. *First, he acknowledged the personal injury, and second, he assigned to God the responsibility for making it right.* Acknowledge the pain when someone hurts you. Assign to God the responsibility to deal with the issue. Insert the name of the person who did you harm.

"_____ has hurt me in many ways.

The Lord will pay them back for what they have done."

Once you've completed this, put the initials "GTDL" next to each resentment of a person who has wronged you. This indicates it is now on "God's To-do List." Remember that forgiving isn't a feeling—it's a choice.

Apply Step Four: I yield my resentments to Christ and choose to forgive those who've wronged me. With every resentment on your list, pray this prayer: "I yield this resentment to you, Lord. I remember how much you've forgiven me. As you've forgiven me, and by the power of your forgiveness, I choose to forgive this person. Thank you for setting me free from the power of this resentment." When you've completed this, you may want to tear the list up and dispose of it.

NOTE: Repeat these four steps as often as necessary.

WHAT ABOUT RECONCILIATION?

It's wonderful when reconciliation takes place. Certainly, pray for reconciliation, and be willing to do your part to bring it about. However, reconciliation may not take place, or it may be delayed many years.

Despite several meetings with the couple mentioned at the start of this chapter, reconciliation did not occur. Three years later, God led us to Southern California. Joanne and I worked through forgiveness, and by God's grace, we moved forward.

Fast-forward seventeen years to 2001. A Sunday was designated as World Reconciliation Day, when believers were encouraged to make restitution, apologize for hurts, and seek to be at peace with one another. Pastors around the world were encouraged to speak on the subject of reconciliation, and I prepared a message on the topic.

As I stood up to speak on reconciliation, I was stunned. Sitting in the fourth or fifth row was the couple who'd inflicted such pain in our lives seventeen years earlier. What were they doing here? They lived nearly 500 miles away, and I couldn't imagine why they'd be in the congregation that day. I certainly didn't want to see them. Strong feelings of hurt and resentment surged through my mind, making it difficult to continue speaking. Knowing they were in the building opened up old wounds and triggered painful memories from the past. Meanwhile, Joanne was feeling her own pain, as this couple was sitting in her row, a few seats away.

I struggled to continue. How could I speak of reconciliation while simultaneously fighting a fierce battle with the issue? This was too close for comfort—too personal. Finally, while delivering the message, I prayed silently, "Lord, I'm willing for reconciliation." Immediately I had the freedom to continue and complete the message.

Later we discovered the couple was visiting Southern California, and they chose a church from the Yellow Pages. God arranged for them to come to Woodbridge Community Church not knowing I was the senior pastor. They were as shocked as we were when they walked in and saw I was the pastor of the church and the speaker for the morning.

Following the service, Joanne and I talked with the couple, and God brought about a spirit of reconciliation. Who but God could have arranged this miraculous meeting on World Reconciliation Sunday more than seventeen years after the conflict?

Two reminders stand out from this God-arranged meeting. First, be ready for reconciliation: sometimes when you least expect it, God will provide an opportunity to bring healing to the relationship. You may see the person in the grocery store or unexpectedly at a wedding. Don't hide or pretend you don't see them. Greet them, and breathe a prayer: "Lord, I'm willing to be reconciled." Be willing to acknowledge your wrongs, and let God take it from there.

Second, resentments that you've dealt with years earlier can resurface. Forgiveness is a lot like peeling an onion, layer after layer, forgiving again and again, and you may shed tears as you peel each layer of the onion. Repeat these four steps as often as needed, daily if necessary.

Step One: I'm powerless to release my resentments.

Step Two: I'm willing for Jesus Christ to set me free from my resentments.

Step Three: I choose to allow God to right this wrong in his time.

Step Four: I yield my resentments to Christ and choose to forgive those who've wronged me.

By choosing to forgive, do you forget the details of the wrong or injustice? No. In most cases, you'll continue to remember the incident. As Jesus Christ brings healing to your life, the day will come when the stinger is removed, the bitterness is absent, and the poison is no longer in your life. One of the famous survivors of the Holocaust, Corrie Ten Boom, wisely stated, "Forgiveness is to set a prisoner free, and to realize that the prisoner was you."

Carrying around a load of bitterness and resentment isn't an indicator of a strong person; it's a sign of weakness, a disabling limp in life. It takes a strong person to forgive. And only God can give you the power to forgive, to turn a debilitating weakness into a display of his strength in your life. This is "turning weakness to strengths."

DAY FIVE—CHAPTER FOUR
TIME OUT

Power Thoughts for Your Time Alone With God

Forgiveness is a lot like peeling an onion, layer after layer, forgiving again and again, and you may shed tears as you peel each layer of the onion.

◊ What resentment do you find most difficult to release? Ask God to work within you to be willing to forgive.

◊ Read Matthew 6:9-15.

◊ Notice that "being forgiven" of your sins requires your willingness to "forgive others" (verse 12).

◊ Further, notice that "not yielding to temptation" and "being rescued from the evil one" (verse 13) are preceded and followed by your willingness to forgive others (vv. 12, 14-15). In what ways are you more vulnerable to temptation when you're holding on to resentment?

◊ Pray through the Lord's Prayer one phrase at a time.

Our Father in heaven, may your name be kept holy.

May your Kingdom come soon.

May your will be done on earth, as it is in heaven.

Give us today the food we need, and forgive us our sins, as we have forgiven those who sin against us.

And don't let us yield to temptation, but rescue us from the evil one. (Matt. 6:9-15 NLT)

TIME TOGETHER

SESSION FOUR

RELEASING RESENTMENTS

Most people attempt to deal with resentments in one of two ways, neither of which works. One method is to bury the resentful feelings by telling yourself, *I'll ignore the pain, and it'll go away sooner or later.* The other approach is to deny the hurt—put on your superman or superwoman cape, pretend to be invincible, and tell yourself, *I'm tough. They tried to hurt me, but there's no way they can get to me, and I'm not going to give them the satisfaction of thinking they can.* In this session, we're going to discover a radically different way to deal with resentments. You'll have the opportunity to walk through four life-changing steps to be set free. Let's get started!

CONNECT

◊ What ticks you off? What are you prone to complain about? Are these triggers the same or different? Do you have a "pet peeve"?

GROW

◊ As a group, read 2 Timothy 4:9-18. Confined in prison, Paul had ample cause to be bitter and resentful. Identify in this passage several things that were potential sources of bitterness for Paul and discuss how he applied a God-perspective. Write them on a poster board and discuss them as a group.

180

Timothy, please come as soon as you can. Demas has deserted me because he loves the things of this life and has gone to Thessalonica. Crescens has gone to Galatia, and Titus has gone to Dalmatia. Only Luke is with me. Bring Mark with you when you come, for he will be helpful to me in my ministry. I sent Tychicus to Ephesus. When you come, be sure to bring the coat I left with Carpus at Troas. Also bring my books, and especially my papers.

Alexander the coppersmith did me much harm, but the Lord will judge him for what he has done. Be careful of him, for he fought against everything we said.

The first time I was brought before the judge, no one came with me. Everyone abandoned me. May it not be counted against them. But the Lord stood with me and gave me strength so that I might preach the Good News in its entirety for all the Gentiles to hear. And he rescued me from certain death. Yes, and the Lord will deliver me from every evil attack and will bring me safely into his heavenly Kingdom. All glory to God forever and ever! Amen. (2 Tim. 4:9-18 NLT)

(If some of the names are too difficult to pronounce, substitute the name with something like "Mr. C" or "Mr. T" or something similar.)

APPLY

◊ Love "keeps no record of wrongs" according to 1 Corinthians 13:5. To assist with understanding what this means in practical terms, think through your answer to each of these statements and have fun discussing them as a group.

1. My "record of wrongs" is erased when someone asks to be forgiven, but not until then.
   Agree   Disagree

2. My "record of wrongs" is effectively eliminated by overlooking the pain and minimizing the hurt.

Agree   Disagree

3. Keeping "no record of wrongs" means the relationship is restored.

Agree   Disagree

4. Keeping "no record of wrongs" means forgetting the offense.

Agree   Disagree

5. Holding on to a resentment makes me more vulnerable to temptation.

Agree   Disagree

◊ Have you experienced victory in forgiving someone? If so, share it with the group.

◊ Read aloud in unison the "Changing My Mind" verse below.

Weed Killer for a Bitter Root

Look after each other
so that none of you fails
to receive the grace of
God. Watch out that no
poisonous root of
bitterness grows up to
trouble you, corrupting
many.
—Heb. 12:15 NLT

◊ Discuss how you can look after each other to prevent bitterness.

PRAY

◊ Commit to remind each other to walk through the steps whenever resentments surface. Close by praying these four steps one at a time. Have someone in the group read Step One, and then spend a brief time in silent prayer, allowing each person to apply this. Then proceed with the other steps, with silent prayer after each one.

Step One: I'm powerless to release my resentments.

Step Two: I'm willing for Jesus Christ to set me free from my resentments.

Step Three: I choose to allow God to right this wrong in his time.

Step Four: I yield my resentments to Christ and choose to forgive those who've wronged me.

◊ It's quite common that one or more individuals in the group may have difficulty releasing resentments. Don't rush the process. As a group, you can gather around them for special prayer, but don't push for or expect an instant release of resentments. Some hurts are very deep; patience and willingness to let them go will bring healing in God's time.

SHARE

◊ Most people like sharing their opinion or expressing what bothers them. Look for an opportunity to start a conversation with someone this week. At an appropriate moment, ask the person a discussion starter like this:

1. What ticks you off? What ignites your fuse?

2. How do you handle it when someone does you wrong?

3. Why do some people hold on to resentments while others release them and move on?

4. What's the key to releasing a resentment?

◊ Look for an opportunity to explain how Jesus Christ set you free from your resentment.

CHAPTER FIVE
RELEASING REGRETS

The prison door to the jail cell of regrets has flung open. Walk out, walk free.

If only I hadn't said …

If only I'd been there for …

If only I hadn't responded the way I did when …

If only I hadn't done what I did …

If only I'd paid attention when …

If you're alive, you inevitably have regrets. Each of us has something we wish we could do over in a different way. The "if only …" tape plays over-and-over again in your mind as a reminder of what could have been, what should have been. Your past drains joy from the present. Living with unresolved regrets is like trying to swim tangled in seaweed. Some regrets are secret, and you may be thinking, *If others knew what I know about me, I'd be finished.* Regrets are chains of self-berating. While resentments have to do with others and forgiving them, regrets have to do with ourselves and accepting God's forgiveness. Regrets and resentments are the ball and chain of an immobilized person.

God never intended that you live your life on a guilt trip, burdened with unresolved regrets. He provides the resources for regret-free living. It's a promise. Living regret-free doesn't mean your memory is erased; instead, the regret no longer controls you and holds you back. You no longer beat yourself up over what happened. Properly processed, regrets have the potential to become high-powered motivation for stronger faith, achievement, and compassion for others. Power in weakness, living a life of surrender, overcomes the grip of regrets. Regrets are a weakness that can be turned into a great strength—God's power point in your life.

TYPES OF REGRETS

I group regrets into three types: 1) embarrassing; 2) painful; and 3) sinful. Of course, there's overlap between the types, which will become obvious.

EMBARRASSING REGRETS

Have any of these things happened to you? Falling on the way to the platform to make a presentation, losing your car in the parking lot, asking a woman who's gained weight when she's expecting, splitting your pants in public, walking into the wrong restroom, falling out of your seat while dozing off in church, getting the hiccups during your wedding ceremony. I'm certain you can add a few.

If you've failed a driver's test, you may not want to tell the world about it but take heart— you're couldn't be more embarrassed than this driver. Mrs. Beatrice Park was taking her fifth driving test. The examination center was in a beautiful location overlooking a river below. She said, "Good morning," to the examiner as he settled into the passenger seat. Flustered, her foot hit the accelerator instead of the clutch, and she panicked. The car shot forward out of the driving test area. Unable to get it under control, the car lurched forward finally nose diving off the embankment and into the swirling river below. As the car sunk in the river, she and the examiner climbed out of the vehicle and waited on the roof to be rescued by helicopter. In a state of shock, the examiner was sent home, still clutching his clipboard. After being rescued, Mrs. Park asked if she'd passed her driving test. She was told, "We can't say until we've seen the examiner's report."[38]

38. Stephen Pile, *The Incomplete Book of Failures* (New York; E. P. Dutton, 1979),

PAINFUL REGRETS

This type of regret isn't necessarily sinful, but it may bring dire consequences and long-term grief. A split-second decision in traffic that injures or kills another person can produce a haunting regret. Making an unwise business decision can have far-reaching ramifications—loss of money, business, home, and family security. These regrets are agonizing—our ideals are shattered as disappointment replaces dreams. Rehearsing what you should have done differently becomes a relentless obsession.

SINFUL REGRETS

Many, if not most, of our regrets are sinful choices that leave a trail of sorrow and shame. Of course, sinful regrets usually include the other two types—sin is embarrassing as well as painful. Sin comes packaged with slick advertising, but underneath it's a big lie, a lie that seduces our cravings and our pride. David's sin, examined in the next section, is a vivid picture of sinful regrets.

DEALING WITH REGRETS: WHAT DOESN'T WORK

Rationalizing or burying regrets may seem like the best strategy to quiet the ghosts of your past. However, no matter how tightly you bolt the door of your memories, the regrets rattle in the closet. They color thinking, imparting a defeatist attitude and a loser's limp and making it more difficult to grow in your Christian faith. You've probably attempted to deal with regrets in one or both of these ways.

BERATING YOURSELF

Depending on the severity of the disappointment, self-berating may become a regular occurrence. The recording plays over-and-over again: *I'm no good. I'm horrible. I'm despicable.*

39–40.

How could I have done what I did? When a believer becomes overwhelmed with feelings of failure, Satan has won a strategic battle. C. S. Lewis said, "Moral collapse follows upon spiritual collapse," and another person said, "It is Satan's strategy to get a Christian preoccupied with their failures; from then on the battle is won."[39]

David journals his inner turmoil and the physical and emotional impact of his sin in this Psalm.

> [3] Because of your anger, my whole body is sick; my health is broken because of my sins. [4] My guilt overwhelms me— it is a burden too heavy to bear. [5] My wounds fester and stink because of my foolish sins. [6] I am bent over and racked with pain. All day long I walk around filled with grief. [7] A raging fever burns within me, and my health is broken. [8] I am exhausted and completely crushed. My groans come from an anguished heart.

> [9] You know what I long for, Lord; you hear my every sigh. [10] My heart beats wildly, my strength fails, and I am going blind. [11] My loved ones and friends stay away, fearing my disease. Even my own family stands at a distance. (Ps. 38:3-11 NLT)

David identified his regrets as a burden too heavy to bear, a highly toxic torment in his body, mind, and spirit. Psychologists and physicians call physical illness caused by mental conditions "psychosomatic illness." Often the cause is deeper. I call it "sin-somatic sickness." While sin does not cause most illnesses, some illnesses and mental conditions are a direct result of sin. From David's lament in Psalm 38, we find potential physical, spiritual, mental, and emotional consequences of unresolved regrets:

Symptoms of Sin-Somatic Sickness

---

39. C. S. Lewis, *God in the Dock*, "Cross-Examination" (1963), paragraph 44, 265. C. S. Lewis is often quoted as saying in *Screwtape Letters*, "It is Satan's strategy to get a Christian preoccupied with their failures; from then on the battle is won." It is a great truth, though it is not found in the *Screwtape Letters*.

Broken health (v. 3)

Feeling overwhelmed, guilt ridden (v. 4)

Festering emotional wounds (v. 5)

Bent over (v. 6)

Depression—filled with grief (v. 6)

Mourning (v. 6)

Searing back pain (v. 7)

Raging fever (v. 7)

Loss of health (v. 7)

Exhausted (v. 8)

Feeling crushed (v. 8)

Groaning (v. 8)

Heart palpitations (v. 10)

Failing strength (v. 10)

Fear of going blind, tired looking eyes (v. 10)

Relational isolation (v. 11)

Though the specific occasion for this Psalm is uncertain, the sin-somatic symptoms may well describe David's condition in the year that followed his sin with Bathsheba. He lusted for her when he saw her bathing. His lust led to adultery, and she became pregnant. In an attempt to cover up the pregnancy, he called her husband, Uriah, home from the battlefield to sleep with his wife. Being a disciplined soldier, Uriah declined this opportunity the first night. The second night, David got him drunk, thinking he would surely go home and have sexual relations with his wife. When this failed, he arranged for Uriah's death on the battlefield. (You can read about it 2 Samuel 11—12.) It was lust, adultery, cover-up, deceit, and murder—and he knew it. That's a heavy load to be hauling around. I don't know what regrets are stuffed away in the closet of your mind, but if David could be set free from his regrets, then there's healing for the stuff that plagues your mind too.

Unresolved regrets will take you down. You get clobbered at the point of your greatest vulnerability. You find yourself on the mat, knocked out, down for the count, wondering what hit you. It's like professional boxer Ralph Walton, who was knocked out in ten and a half seconds in a boxing match in Lewiston, Maine. When the bell rang to begin the first round, his opponent, Al Couture, darted across the ring and swung at Walton before he'd left his corner. The ten and a half seconds included the ten seconds while he was counted out. Ralph was on his feet for a grand total of one-half second. With unresolved regrets, when a big challenge and a unique opportunity comes up, you may be knocked out of action before you know what hit you.

DAY ONE—CHAPTER FIVE

TIME OUT

Power Thoughts for Your Time Alone With God

Living with unresolved regrets is like trying to swim tangled in seaweed.

◊ In your own words, describe what it's like to live with an unresolved regret.

◊ Read the account of David in 2 Samuel 11:1-27.

◊ What does this statement mean to you? "I don't know what regrets are stuffed away in the closet of your mind, but if David could be set free from his regrets, then there's healing for the stuff you regret too."

◊ Go to the back of your book for this week's meditation verse titled "Blameless." Carry it with you or put it someplace where you can direct your thoughts to it throughout the day and memorize it.

BLAMING OTHERS

The "shame game"—berating yourself—is different from the "blame game"—berating others. A blaming person may be unaware of their critical spirit; all the while, however, it is quite obvious to others. Those who are closest bear the brunt of the blame: a sharp, cutting tongue, subtle putdowns. The Psalmist observed, "Your mouth is filled with wickedness, and your tongue is full of lies. You sit around and slander your brother—your own mother's son" (Ps. 50:19-20 NLT). If your regrets weigh heavily, you'll be prone to offset this by blaming others. Strangely, the flaws of others provide temporary mental relief from personal failures and disappointments. Guilt and blame work like a scale in your soul. When you feel guilty, the natural tendency is to be critical of others. Blaming them seems to help in restoring the equilibrium. I share this weakness with St. Augustine, who said, "O Lord, deliver me from this lust of always vindicating myself." It's the art of excusing ourselves by blaming the other person—something we inherited from our great grandparents, Adam and Eve.

It's a whole lot easier to blame others when they really are at fault. The more blame you can come up with, the less guilty you feel. This will prevent you from seeing your share in the problem.

The crowd must have gone hysterical with the humorous hyperbole in this warning by Jesus about being judgmental:

"Do not judge others, and you will not be judged. For you will be treated as you treat others. The standard you use in judging is the standard by which you will be judged.

"And why worry about a speck in your friend's eye when you have a log in your own? How can you think of saying to your friend, 'Let me help you get rid of that speck in your eye,' when you can't see past the log in your own eye? Hypocrite! First get rid of the log in your own eye; then you will see well enough to deal with the speck in your friend's eye. (Mt. 7:1-5 NLT)

Use your imagination with this scene. This guy is walking around with an enormous plank sticking out of his eye. Meandering through life, he hauls this big piece of timber around, banging into things and looking weird to everyone. What does the world look like for "Mr. Log-in-the-eye"? It looks like a gigantic forest. What's in his eye is all he can see. Everywhere he turns, he sees wood, timber, logs. No wonder the speck in the other person's eye looks like an enormous log. Personal guilt magnifies the faults of others, distorting them all out of perspective. The apostle Paul cautioned, "Therefore you have no excuse, everyone of you who passes judgment, for in that which you judge another, you condemn yourself; for you who judge practice the same things" (Rom. 2:1).

I'm grateful to my parents for many things they imparted to me, including hard work, honesty, and moral values. On the flip side, my childhood home was a highly toxic and unhealthy emotional environment. Anger, hostility, and fights were frequent events for the eighteen years I lived at home. Many nights I went to sleep listening to the latest Mom-Dad fight getting out of control upstairs. It would go on for a half-hour or more, and then I'd hear the physical pushing, shoving, and hitting.

When I was in seventh grade, I got in the middle of a fight involving my dad and mom. He pushed her, and she fell. I jumped in, and Dad turned on me. I headed for the stairs to the basement, and he continued after me with his belt swinging wildly. One of the blows caused me to fall down the stairs and land on the concrete floor where I ended up bleeding and bruised. I ran from the house and found some cigarettes and started smoking. Somehow smoking numbed the seething anger. Most kids start smoking as a social dare, something they do to be cool and fit in with the crowd. For me, this was never the case. When I smoked, I was always alone and isolated in rage and resentment. This was the era of the "dirty five Christian don'ts": don't go to movies, drink alcohol, play cards, dance, or smoke. To me, smoking was worse than all the others. The result was agonizing shame, but when the anger and pain became too much, I resorted to numbing it. This continued off and on in the years that followed. Even though it was a rare occurrence, it was a deep regret and something I hoped no one would ever know. This led to hypocrisy and dishonesty, which was probably worse. For me, this was a deep-seated regret, loaded with shame, embarrassment, and disappointment. The easy thing to do would be to blame my parents, but this behavior was my own responsibility.

DAY TWO—CHAPTER FIVE

TIME OUT

Power Thoughts for Your Time Alone With God

O Lord, deliver me from this lust of always vindicating myself.
—Augustine

◊ Identify when you've played the blame game. What was going on inside you?

◊ Read 1 Timothy 1:12-20. Paul describes himself as a blasphemer, persecutor, a violent man, and the worst of sinners. Paul was a terrorist before coming to Christ, and the searing memory of putting Christians to death must never have left his mind. Christ's complete forgiveness transformed Paul's life, and it will transform yours as well.

◊ You'll find it helpful to write down your regrets so they can be processed and released. Be specific. Identify actions, attitudes, words spoken, or things you failed to do. Use the Releasing Regrets (Appendix D) in the back of the book or a separate sheet of paper you can destroy later.

DEALING WITH REGRETS: WHAT WORKS

The word "agree" is a crucial word in dealing with regrets. It means to "bring something or someone into agreement; to harmonize, to reconcile." God wants you to be reconciled with him, to harmonize your relationship, to establish an agreement or understanding. There are four aspects to this God-agreement, the source of regret-free living.

First, agree with God about your regrets.

Listen as God speaks.

> Come, let's talk this over, says the Lord; no matter how deep the stain of your sins, I can take it out and make you as clean as freshly fallen snow. Even if you are stained as red as crimson, I can make you white as wool! (Isa. 1:18 TLB)

> People who conceal their sins will not prosper, but if they confess and turn from them, they will receive mercy. (Prov. 28:13 NLT)

> I confess my sins; I am deeply sorry for what I have done. (Ps. 38:18 NLT)

> If we confess our sins to him, he is faithful and just to forgive us our sins and to cleanse us from all wickedness. (1 John 1:9 NLT)

Don't rush past these verses. I suggest reading them again to get the full impact. Express your willingness to agree with your Creator. *You're right, God. I blew it. I sinned. I messed up. I was wrong. I failed.* The Greek word for "confess" in 1 John 1:9 means to "say the same thing as" or "agree with." Distress that drives us to God is for our benefit. "It turns us around. It gets us back in the way of salvation. We never regret that kind of pain. But those who let distress drive them away from God are full of regrets and end up on a deathbed of regrets" (2 Cor. 7:10 MSG).

Sins are forgiven at the moment of salvation, but sinful behavior breaks fellowship with God. Confession is agreeing with God and seeking a new direction, thus renewing the intimacy of our relationship. Some assume confessing sin requires shedding tears and becoming emotionally distraught. This may occur, but it's not required to simply agree with God.

SECOND, AGREE WITH GOD REGARDING THOSE YOU'VE HURT.

Jesus said if you come to offer your gift in worship and remember someone has something against you, be reconciled with that person first and then come and offer your gift. "So when you offer your gift to God at the altar, and you remember that your brother or sister has something against you, leave your gift there at the altar. Go and make peace with that person, and then come and offer your gift" (Matt. 5:23-24 NCV).

The key phrase is "you remember that your brother or sister has something against you." Who do you need to be reconciled with? Your spouse, your parents or children, someone in the workplace, a neighbor? The verse says, "Go and make peace." This is a straightforward command. Go immediately and say, "I was wrong when I _____, and I want to ask for your forgiveness. Will you forgive me?" If you defrauded the person, make restitution by repaying what was stolen. Be careful not to indict the other person by blaming them in your apology. Don't say, "I'm sorry I yelled at you, but you made me so angry when you made that statement." Simply state the wrong: "I was wrong to yell at you. Please forgive me."

Zacchaeus had a life of regrets to deal with when he came to Jesus. He was a chief tax collector in the region of Jericho, and he'd become very rich cheating people. Tax collectors were considered traitors since they served the Roman government, and they were notorious for their dishonesty. As a result, they were expelled from the synagogue, and they couldn't serve as witnesses or as judges. They epitomized the term "filthy rich"— and they were despised.

When Jesus visited Jericho, short-of-stature Zacchaeus climbed a sycamore-fig tree to see Jesus over the crowd. Since he was considered a traitor, people in the crowd probably didn't want to associate with this slime anyway. I would imagine if he were among the crowd, someone would have jabbed him hard in the ribs, stepped on his toes, or given him a push. Jesus saw Zacchaeus up in the tree and announced he was going to his house that day. A remarkable change took place in Zacchaeus. The Scripture says, "Zacchaeus stood before the Lord and said, 'I will give half my wealth to the poor, Lord, and if I have cheated people on their taxes, I will give them back four times as much!'" (Luke 19:8 NLT).

After his encounter with Jesus, I can imagine a Jewish family seeing Zacchaeus coming up the road to their house. "Oh, no! Here comes that blood-sucking tax collector to get money out of us and cheat us again." Zacchaeus knocks on the door and says, "Sorry to bother you, but I'm here with your tax refund. I'm returning the amount I cheated you out of, and I'm including 400 percent interest on the amount as well. Have a nice day." The reaction must have been astounding—dropped jaws, fainting spells, total disbelief. Who knows? Once they recovered from the shock, they may have invited Zach in for supper with the family. Zacchaeus was being set free from his regretful life.

When you ask forgiveness from another person, you have an impact on their "guilt-blame" balance. They may have been justifying their actions by blaming you. When you humble yourself and ask forgiveness, they suddenly become aware of their wrong in the situation. Don't count on it, but it's not uncommon for them to respond, "I was wrong as well. I ask your forgiveness for my part in this." This sort of action leads to the sweetness of reconciliation.

What if the other person doesn't have something against you? Years ago, Joanne felt she was obligated to apologize for negative thoughts she had about another girl. The girl didn't have a clue that Joanne felt this way about her so when Joanne apologized, the girl was shocked and hurt. If what you confess may be more hurtful than helpful, check with someone you trust before proceeding. Should a man tell a woman who is totally unaware of his thoughts, "I confess having lustful thoughts about you"? No!

DAY THREE—CHAPTER FIVE

TIME OUT

Power Thoughts for Your Time Alone With God

Cling to your faith in Christ, and keep your conscience clear. For some people have deliberately violated their consciences; as a result, their faith has been shipwrecked.—1 Tim. 1:19 NLT

◊ Read Matthew 5:23-24 and Acts 16:24.

◊ Ask God to bring to mind people you've wronged. If these aren't on your list of regrets you wrote on day two, add them now. Take steps now to contact these people—in person, by phone, or if necessary, in a letter—and humbly ask, "Will you forgive me?" Put a check in the "apology" column when you've completed this.

Third, agree with God regarding his forgiveness.

You've likely heard someone say, "You need to forgive yourself." Is this biblical? Is it humanly possible?

I wish I had the name of the woman I met at a conference who challenged my thinking on this point. At the breakfast table, when the topic of forgiving yourself came up, she asked, "Is it humanly possible to forgive yourself?" I didn't reply immediately sensing she had an insight to share. She stated her opinion that, in most cases, forgiving yourself is humanly impossible. My mind immediately began to think through verses on the subject. *Hmm ... Is there a verse in the Bible that tells me to forgive myself?* I couldn't think of one, but the Scripture does say to forgive your enemies. So if you're your own worst enemy, I guess that would include forgiving yourself.

As I thought about her point, I realized this is where people get stuck. They try to forgive themselves, but they discover the harder they try, the deeper the feelings of regret. Forgiveness requires God's intervention. Rather than struggling to forgive yourself, agree with God and accept his forgiveness. If God— the Creator of the Universe, the ultimate judge of all, the one who night and day is surrounded by angels saying, "Holy, holy, holy is the Lord God Almighty"—chooses to forgive you, then who are you to doubt what he has done? Accept his forgiveness. This is the *only* way to appropriate true forgiveness of yourself. How could we possibly come before God's throne if our sins weren't totally forgiven? Trying to forgive yourself is a human effort of the flesh—futile and incomplete. Accepting God's forgiveness as your forgiveness is an act of faith, and without faith it's impossible to please God (Heb. 11:6).

God not only forgives, but he also forgets. "I will forgive their iniquity, and their sin I will remember no more" (Jer. 31:34). What? How could God forget? Is God absent-minded or forgetful? No. He *chooses* to forget, to remember your sins no more. Max Lucado said it this way: "God doesn't just forgive, he forgets. He erases the board. He destroys the evidence. He burns the microfilm. He clears the computer. He doesn't remember my mistakes."[40]

Because you're in Christ, God accepts you as blameless, without a single fault (Eph. 1:4). Christ died for you that he might "holy and blameless as you stand before him without a single fault" (Col. 1:22 NLT). Hebrews 4:16 invites us to "… draw near with confidence to the throne of grace, so that we may receive mercy and find grace to help in time of need." If God hadn't forgiven and forgotten your failings, how could you come into his holy presence?

God's forgiveness as well as his choice not to remember your sins is woven throughout the Scriptures. Allow these verses to grip you:

> For his unfailing love toward those who fear him is as great as the height of the heavens above the earth. He has removed our sins as far from us as the east is from the west. (Ps. 103:11-12 NLT)

> It was for my own good that I had such hard times. But your love protected me from doom in the deep pit, and you turned your eyes away from my sins. (Is. 38:17 CEV)

> Once again you will have compassion on us. You will trample our sins under your feet and throw them into the depths of the ocean! (Mic. 7:19 NLT)

> "I—yes, I alone—will blot out your sins for my own sake and will never think of them again. (Is. 43:25 NLT)

> "Therefore repent and return, so that your sins may be wiped away, in order that times of refreshing may come from the presence of the Lord. (Acts 3:19)

---

40. Max Lucado, *God Came Near* (Portland: Multnomah Press, 1987), 73.

My dear children, I am writing this to you so that you will not sin. But if anyone does sin, we have an advocate who pleads our case before the Father. He is Jesus Christ, the one who is truly righteous. (1 John 2:1 NLT)

Does your memory of a regrettable behavior disappear? In most cases, no. You will still be able to recall the incident. When the memory of a past failure comes to the surface, simply remember this: *God forgives and forgets.* Thank him for his forgiveness and intentional forgetfulness. It's settled, done. Bolt the door on haunting memories in your mental closet.

DAY FOUR—CHAPTER FIVE

TIME OUT

Power Thoughts for Your Time Alone With God

If God—the Creator of the Universe, the ultimate judge of all, the one who night and day is surrounded by angels saying, "Holy, holy, holy is the LORD God Almighty"—chooses to forgive you, then who are you to doubt what God has done? Accept his forgiveness.

◊ Read James 5:13-20.

◊ The word "confess" in James 5:16 is essentially the same as "confess" in 1 John 1:9 (both come from the same Greek word meaning "to agree with, to say one and the same thing"). The word for "confess" in James 5:16 has a prefix with it meaning "to confess out, to express verbally." James is saying, "Agree with God and another person about your sins and faults and ask them to pray for your healing."

◊ Do you have a close friend to share your regrets with? God promises healing from "confessing our sins to one another." If you share with your small group, they must be committed to absolute confidentiality. There may be some regrets that are deeply personal, and you may not feel open to share them with the group. Instead, ask God for a mature and understanding believer to be your prayer partner. Some issues may need to be processed with a Christian counselor or pastor.

Fourth, agree with God regarding his future for you.

Set free from regrets, you can look to a bright future. "For I know the plans I have for you," says the LORD. "They are plans for good and not for disaster, to give you a future and a hope" (Jer. 29:11 NLT).

The prison doors to the jail cell of condemnation and regrets have flung open. Walk out, walk free. "Therefore there is now no condemnation for those who are in Christ Jesus" (Rom. 8:1). Now run the race without being tripped up. Hebrews 12:1-2 says, "Let us strip off every weight that slows us down, especially the sin that so easily trips us up. And let us run with endurance the race God has set before us. We do this by keeping our eyes on Jesus" (NLT). Sin will entangle and trip you up, but what is the weight that slows you down? I believe the weight is self-condemnation, guilt, and shame. Strip off the weight of regrets and run the race with God-confidence.

What can you do to safeguard your future from regrets? First, when you sin, be quick to confess your sin—agree with God—and then move forward by casting off the weight of self-condemnation. Second, do an inventory of potential "regret ruts" you tend to get into. What behaviors need to be checked or abandoned? What decisions need to be made now to prevent future regrets? Ask God for his guidance. "The LORD says, 'I will guide you along the best pathway for your life. I will advise you and watch over you. Do not be like a senseless horse or mule that needs a bit and bridle to keep it under control'" (Ps. 32:8-9 NLT).

Deal with stubbornness. Choose wise behavior. For example, choose to safeguard your marriage. Don't allow yourself to be alone with a member of the opposite sex in an inappropriate setting. This is a regret safeguard. As noted earlier, not all regrets are sinful behavior. Some are safety and good sense issues. Live your life making safe choices. Allow some margins in your schedule so you don't drive at break-neck speeds to get somewhere. This is a safeguard against a needless accident.

I hate losing stuff—leaving my sunglasses or my jacket somewhere because I was in a hurry or forgetful. My goal for this year: "Don't lose anything but a few extra pounds." As a discipline, I attempt to make a careful check before leaving a location. Think behaviors through in advance. Study the regrets others experience. You don't have to experience every regret yourself; you're not missing anything. Have you ever heard anyone make these statements?

"I regret eating right and taking care of my body."

"I regret never experimenting with illegal drugs."

"I regret wearing a seatbelt and choosing to drive safely."

"I regret saving myself for my marriage partner."

I have *never* heard anyone make any of these statements. Making wise choices now can prevent future "regret ruts."

WHEN A REGRET RESURFACES

You may find that even though you experience release from a regret, it may be re-triggered by a memory or something someone says. This is particularly true when someone will not forgive you and continues to bring up your failure. Also, Satan is your accuser (Rev. 12:10), and he will taunt you with your past sins and failures. Take these three steps whenever regrets return.

FIRST, PICTURE YOURSELF DECLARED BLAMELESS IN THE PRESENCE OF GOD.

Stop thinking about your regret. Rather than letting it take over your mind, "resist the devil and he will flee from you" (James 4:7). Don't fight it; replace it. The verse for meditation this week is powerful. God has declared you blameless in his sight. Add some of the other verses mentioned in this chapter and write them on cards to carry with you. Memorize one or several to focus on when a regretful thought returns.

Second, don't get frustrated trying to forgive yourself.

This is relying on human strength. Ask yourself, *Who am I to argue with God?* Remember, forgiveness is simply agreeing with God. You can't earn forgiveness. It's God's love gift for you. Listen to God speak and accept his forgiveness.

Third, remember you're completely forgiven and forever loved.

My mother was constantly overwhelmed with the wonder of God's extravagant grace. In a tribute to her life, I wrote this for her memorial service. Today I carry this in my personal growth notebook and refer to it often, particularly when I'm disappointed in myself.

Forever Loved

God loves me with an everlasting love, and I am forgiven
and forever set free from condemnation and judgment.
God through Christ has made me holy and blameless,
and there is nothing I can do to improve my standing
before God. As Christ was crucified and resurrected, I am
crucified with him and resurrected with him, giving me
power over sin and newness of life. God's amazing grace
freely paid the price for my sin, granting me the gift of
eternal life
… forever, forever, forever, and forever!

LEVERAGING REGRETS

Georgia Tech and the University of California squared off for the big football game on New Year's Day, 1929, in the Rose Bowl. Prior to the end of the first half, Roy Riegels recovered a fumble for California, but then to everyone's shock, he became confused and ran in the wrong direction. Fortunately, before scoring for Georgia Tech, a teammate named Benny Lom chased him down the field and tackled him. The mistake of Roy Riegels cost his team sixty-five yards, and California was forced to kick. Georgia Tech blocked the punt and scored a safety, which proved to be the final margin of victory for Georgia Tech.

In the dressing room at half-time, Riegels sat in a corner staring at the floor with a blanket around his shoulders. With his face in his hands, the big football player began to sob. Coach Price said little as he pondered the question on everyone's mind: *Should I play Riegels in the second half?* At the three-minute announcement, Coach Price said, "Men, the same team that played the first half will start the second." As the players filed out of the dressing room, Riegels remained in his corner, feeling like a failure to himself and the team. The coach came over and said, "Roy, didn't you hear me? The same team that played the first half will start the second." With his cheeks wet with tears, Roy looked up and said, "Coach, I can't do it to save my life. I've ruined you. I've ruined myself. I couldn't face that crowd in the stadium to save my life." Coach Price put a hand on his shoulder and said, "Roy, get up and go on back; the game is only half over." Riegels went back, and the Georgia Tech players would testify that no one played a tougher game of football in the second half than Roy Riegels.[41]

---

41. Haddon W. Robinson, "The Gospel of the Second Chance," *Moody Monthly* (February 1979), 71–72.

Are you ready for the second half? The failures and regrets in your past are over. You can't change them, but you can release them. Allow your past failures to motivate you.

Regrets have positive potential—a hidden, camouflaged benefit. From regrets, you become aware of your own weakness, learn compassion for others who fail, and develop stronger faith. Filled with gratitude, live your remaining days running full-throttle for God. Turn the weakness of your regrets into tender compassion for others and an unwavering commitment to Christ.

David's sin was shameful, scandalous, and he was miserable carrying around his heavy load of regrets—lust, adultery, cover-up, deceit, and murder. Dragging himself through life with searing back pain, loss of health, feeling feeble and crushed with heart palpitations and failing strength, the sparkle gone from his eyes, overwhelmed with festering wounds, depressed, mourning, and groaning, David was a miserable mess.

What changed everything? David accepted God's forgiveness as his forgiveness. Regrets will cause you to run *from* God or run *to* God. Many believe King David wrote Psalm 71. If so, it's likely he wrote it near the end of his life. The Psalmist exclaims, "I run for dear life to GOD, I'll never live to regret it" (Ps. 71:1 MSG). God's evaluation of David: "God removed Saul and replaced him with David, a man about whom God said, 'I have found David son of Jesse, a man after my own heart. He will do everything I want him to do'" (Acts 13:22 NLT).

What is the deep, shameful regret that rattles in the closet of your mind? Release it, and accept God's full, unconditional forgiveness. Don't argue with God. Simply agree with his forgiveness.

David hit bottom in agonizing shame. But he didn't stay there. God flung the prison door to the jail cell of regrets wide open, and David walked out—free. He became a man after

God's own heart. David's words live on, words for you in this life-changing moment—your moment to find release from the prison of regrets.

If you make a run for God—you won't regret it! —Ps. 2:12 MSG

DAY FIVE—CHAPTER FIVE

TIME OUT

Power Thoughts for Your Time Alone With God

God loves me with an everlasting love, and I am forgiven and forever set free from condemnation and judgment.

◊ Read Psalm 51:1-19.

◊ Complete the "My Agreeing with God Agreement" which follows. You are set free. Destroy the list you made earlier.

MY AGREEING WITH GOD AGREEMENT

Lord Jesus, let's talk about my regrets. You died on the cross to purchase the forgiveness of all my sins. You paid the price in full. I agree with you regarding my regrets. I blew it. I was wrong. I messed up. I acknowledge and confess my sin. Rather than trying to forgive myself, I will accept your forgiveness as my forgiveness.

You promised, "I—yes, I alone—will blot out your sins for my own sake and will never think of them again" (Is. 43:25 NLT). You wipe the slate clean, you erase my regrets, you remove them as far as the east is from the west, and you bury them in the deepest sea with a sign that says, "No fishing."

Thank you that you forgive, and you forget. I completely accept and acknowledge your forgiveness. When I fail in the future, which will certainly occur, I will confess and then immediately agree with you and accept your forgiveness.

Fill me with the Holy Spirit and empower me to live my remaining days with compassion and understanding for others and a deep desire to serve you.

Thank you for your eternal forgetfulness. Right now I join David in a forgiveness celebration: Oh, what joy for those whose disobedience is forgiven, whose sin is put out of sight! Yes, what joy for those whose record the LORD has cleared of guilt, whose lives are lived in complete honesty! (Ps. 32:1-2 NLT).

_____   _____
Signed   Date

TIME TOGETHER

SESSION FIVE

RELEASING REGRETS

Releasing regrets is the flipside to releasing resentments, the focus of our last session. While resentments have to do with others and forgiving them, regrets have to do with you and accepting God's forgiveness. If you're alive, you inevitably have regrets, things you wish you could do over in a different way. In this session, we're going to celebrate with David the Psalmist: "What happiness for those whose guilt has been forgiven! What joys when sins are covered over! What relief for those who have confessed their sins and God has cleared their record" (Ps. 32:1 TLB). Let the celebration begin!

CONNECT

◊ As a group, share how you'd complete this phrase: "If only ..." Your response may be lighthearted: "If only I'd set the timer when I put the roast in the oven ..." or more serious: "If only I'd kept my mouth shut when ..."

GROW

◊ Read aloud as a group 2 Samuel 11:1-17.

◊ Imagine yourselves as a reporter for *The Jerusalem Times*, and you're interviewing David toward the close of his life. What do you think his responses would be? (Or have someone role-play being David.)

216

Question #1: David, how did covering up your sin backfire in your life?

Question #2: How did your personal failings affect your relationship with God, your family, and other people?

Question #3: How did it affect your relationship with Bathsheba when she became your wife? Did she ever use this against you?

Question #4: How did you feel after the Bathsheba affair? How was your physical, mental, and emotional health affected?

Question #5: How did you become a man after God's own heart?

APPLY

◊ As a group, discuss your "regret safeguards" in these areas. These may include safety and good sense decisions as well as moral and integrity issues.

1. Health Safeguards

2. Safety Safeguards

3. Family Safeguards

4. Moral and Integrity Safeguards

5. Financial Safeguards

◊ Read aloud in unison the "Changing My Mind" verse for this week.

Blameless

Even before he made
the world, God loved
us
and chose us in Christ
to be holy and
without fault in his
eyes.
—Eph. 1:4 NLT

PRAYER AND COMMUNION

◊ Read these verses from Psalm 51 as a group. Pause after each group of verses to allow for brief, silent prayer.

Have mercy on me, O God, because of your unfailing love. Because of your great compassion, blot out the stain of my sins. Wash me clean from my guilt. Purify me from my sin.

Oh, give me back my joy again; you have broken me— now let me rejoice. Don't keep looking at my sins. Remove the stain of my guilt. Create in me a clean heart, O God. Renew a loyal spirit within me.

The sacrifice you desire is a broken spirit. You will not reject a broken and repentant heart, O God. (Ps. 51:1-2, 8-10, 17 NLT)

◊ Slowly read aloud the "My Agreeing with God Agreement" on the next page, and then sign it.

MY AGREEING WITH GOD AGREEMENT

Lord Jesus, let's talk about my regrets. You died on the cross to purchase the forgiveness of all my sins. You paid the price in full. I agree with you regarding my regrets. I blew it. I was wrong. I messed up. I acknowledge and confess my sin. Rather than trying to forgive myself, I will accept your forgiveness as my forgiveness.

You promised, "I—yes, I alone—will blot out your sins for my own sake and will never think of them again" (Is. 43:25 NLT). You wipe the slate clean, you erase my regrets, you remove them as far as the east is from the west, and you bury them in the deepest sea with a sign that says, "No fishing."

Thank you that you forgive, and you forget. I completely accept and acknowledge your forgiveness. When I fail in the future, which will certainly occur, I will confess and then immediately agree with you and accept your forgiveness.

Fill me with the Holy Spirit and empower me to live my remaining days with compassion and understanding for others and a deep desire to serve you.

Thank you for your eternal forgetfulness. Right now I join David in a forgiveness celebration: Oh, what joy for those whose disobedience is forgiven, whose sin is put out of sight! Yes, what joy for those whose record the LORD has cleared of guilt, whose lives are lived in complete honesty! (Ps. 32:1-2 NLT).

_____

Signed   Date

◊ Together, share communion (sometimes called "The Lord's Supper" or "The Eucharist," which means "to give thanks"). Churches often have different traditions about how communion should be served, but this is a simple procedure that works well in a small group.

Suggested Preparation and Procedure for Serving Communion in a Small Group

1. Have a loaf of bread or matzo crackers along with a goblet of juice prepared and ready.

2. The group leader reads 1 Corinthians 11:23-26 and leads in prayer, thanking the Lord Jesus for his broken body and shed blood, which cleanses from all sin.

3. One way to serve communion is for each group member to serve another member. The leader takes the bread and tears off a portion. Turning to the person on their right, the leader says, "This represents the body of Christ broken for you." This person takes the bread, tears off a portion, and holds it until the juice is passed. They then turn to the person on their right and say, "This represents the body of Christ broken for you." Proceed around the group, with everyone holding the bread until the juice is served.

4. The leader takes the goblet of juice. Turning to the person on their right, the leader says, "This represents the blood of Christ shed for you." The person takes the goblet, dips the bread in it, and eats the bread. They present the goblet to the person on their right, and say, "This represents the blood of Christ shed for you." Proceed around the group. The leader is the last to be served.

5. As an alternative, the group leader may serve communion to each person.

6. Close by singing "Amazing Grace" or another appropriate song.

7. As a group, discuss doing a deed of kindness or giving a love gift for a needy person or family this week.

SHARE

◊ How do you open the door to share your faith? Learn the fine art of asking a thought-provoking question. Look for wthe opportunity to get a conversation started this week using these questions:

1. Is it possible to live regret free?

2. What hope is there for a person who's unable to forgive themselves?

3. Is it possible to forgive yourself?

CHAPTER SIX

FIXIN' THE WEAKNESSES IN OTHERS?

*Differences are the sandpaper God uses to polish
the rough edges of our character.*

What do I do about the weaknesses of others, particularly when their flaws are driving me nuts? Do I scold, lecture, nag, or avoid them? Whether it's a relationship with a friend, co-worker, college roommate, or family member, weaknesses and differences can be a major source of frustration. If you're in the same household with an opposite, how do you maintain sanity when differences grate and irritate? This is the jagged edginess of relationships.

Does it work to try to change someone? Is it possible? Is there a way to cooperate with God as he works to change someone? Let's look at principles to be an agent for change—whether work, school, sports, church, or small group. Strengths and weaknesses play a big part in the success or failure of a relationship.

COMPATIBILITY

It's a good idea to identify some degree of compatibility before selecting a college roommate, a friend to rent an apartment with, or a marriage partner. Some colleges and universities now attempt to match dorm roommates based on sleep and study habits, room temperature, likes and dislikes. With the increase in divorce due to irreconcilable differences, perhaps applicants for a marriage license should complete a "compatibility quiz." A simple test could be devised to check for agreeable temperament in such matters as noise tolerance level, messiness or tidiness,

nocturnal tendencies, eating habits, mean room temperature ...
and general meanness. I decided to have some fun with this so
here's my quiz to kick things off.

COMPATIBILITY QUIZ

(Check all that apply)

1. ___Snores at night; ___Complains about those who snore;
___Talks in sleep; ___Walks in sleep; ___Wheezes in sleep

2. ___Answers phone immediately; ___Unplugs the phone;
___Yells for others to answer the phone

3. ___Reads in bed; ___Clips fingernails in bed; ___Sleeps
in bed; ___Eats in bed; ___Hoards covers in bed; ___Flosses
teeth in bed

4. ___Doesn't like pets; ___Likes some pets; ___Feeds the
dog at the table; ___Bathes with the dog; ___Doesn't bathe with
the dog, but bathes less frequently than the dog

5. ___Wants things neat and clean; ___Tidy, but not super
neat; ___Three years behind on spring cleaning; ___Thinks dust
is decorative

6. ___Listens to elevator music; ___Likes country music;
___Likes anything with lots of volume; ___Addicted to silence;
___Thinks earbuds are jewelry; ___Listens to stereo, watches
TV, reads newspaper while listening to spouse

7. Interval for bathroom stops on vacation: ___10 minutes;
___30 minutes; ___2 hours; ___4 hours; ___2 days

8. Electric blanket setting: ___1; ___4; ___7; ___10 with 3
quilts, thermostat on 78

9. ___Eager to get up before the sun gets up; ___Eager to get up before the sun sets

10. Arrival time for events: ___5 to 15 minutes early; ___30 seconds early; ___5 to 15 minutes late; ___Thinks departure and arrival times are the same; ___Enjoys being late to make a "grand entrance"[42]

While this is in jest, it strikes a serious note. The issues underlying compatibility are serious stuff. Bottom line: *God designed every person with weaknesses as well as vastly different likes and dislikes.* For example, it's normal for brothers and sisters—raised in the same household with the same parents, the same value system and training—to have uniquely different personalities and temperaments, respond differently to the training, and go different directions in life.

Nationally recognized personal development speaker and writer Earl Nightingale shared this research in an article titled "How to React to Stress."

> Two young boys were raised by an alcoholic father. As they grew older, they moved away from that broken home, each going his own way in the world. Several years later, they happened to be interviewed separately by a psychologist who was analyzing the effects of drunkenness on children in broken homes. His research revealed that the two men were strikingly different from each other. One was a clean-living teetotaler; the other, a hopeless drunk like his father. The psychologist asked each of them why he developed the way he did, and each gave an identical answer, "What else would you expect when you have a father like mine?"[43]

---

42. Adapted from Dave Beckwith, "The Ultimate Compatibility Quiz," *Marriage Partnership*, Fall 1991, 37.
43. This was quoted by Earl Nightingale, "How to React to Stress," Nightingale-Conant, 1400 South Wolf Road, Bldg. 300, Suite 103, Wheeling, IL 60090. The research was originally done by Dr. Hans Selye, Canadian physician and scientist who pioneered stress research.

If you're a parent with more than one child, are your children different from each other? I'm sure you've discovered differences in their temperaments and weaknesses in their character. Just when moms and dads think they're getting the first child figured out, along comes the second one. And they find themselves thinking, *Where did this one come from? This one must be your child. He or she is a total opposite of me.*

Personally, I think God should have started us out with grandchildren. You know, have them over for the weekend and see how it goes. On Sunday afternoon, pack their stuff up and send them back to their parents who are highly qualified because they received their five-year grandparent apprentice training before becoming "real parents." This would allow potential moms and dads to sharpen some parenting skills and develop a clear-cut game plan before having children of their own. Instead, God gives inexperienced, naïve parents a predesigned little bundle of mischief stamped "no refund, no return," and says, "See if you can figure this one out."

God could have designed us without weaknesses. God also could have designed everyone perfectly compatible—sleeping and waking up at the same time, liking the same foods, enjoying the same music, amused by the same jokes, fancying the same colors. How boring! God, the Creator, is creative. He designs each person with meticulous detail; no two people have the same fingerprint or DNA. Differences are God's signature indicating, "You're one of a kind; you're special." Why, other than being infinitely creative, did God design people differently? Weaknesses in others and differences in likes and dislikes are the sandpaper God uses to polish the rough edges of our character.

DAY ONE—CHAPTER SIX
TIME OUT

Power Thoughts for Your Time Alone With God

*Differences are God's signature saying, "You're one of a kind—
you're special."*

◊ Read Romans 12:6–16. Identify and underline key phrases in this passage for loving, understanding, and appreciating others.

◊ Chart your profile of strengths and weaknesses, along with those of your spouse or close friend.

Your Profile

Strengths	Weaknesses

Their Profile

Strengths	Weaknesses

◊ How did God design you differently than the person you're closest to? In what ways are your talents, gifts, and skills different? What do you appreciate about that person? Have you told them so?

◊ Go to the back of your book for this week's meditation verse titled "Accept One Another." Carry it with you or put it someplace where you can direct your thoughts to it throughout the day and memorize it.

MIXING AND MATCHING

The closeness of a family relationship best illustrates weaknesses and differences that can cause friction. These principles are at play in virtually all relationships.

Jerry and Alice had been married for nineteen years and needed few reminders that they were opposites. Jerry was a high-energy, athletic, outgoing, optimistic forty-six-year-old. Early to bed, early to rise, he could outwork and outrun most men half his age or half-again his size. Highly disciplined and meticulous about what he ate, he scolded others for eating "junk foods." His wife, Alice, was quiet, reserved, and cautious, with a melancholy sweetness. Meeting people was difficult and awkward for Alice, but those who took the time to get to know her discovered a kind, resourceful, and refreshing person. Alice was sensitive, caring, and compassionate. She'd nurse a wounded stray kitten for weeks or work until two a.m. to put together the costume for her daughter's school play. Jerry was fun to meet, with his quick wit and bubbly personality. Alice made friends slowly but developed intense loyalty. She was sluggish through most of the day but came alive about eight p.m.—just when Jerry was winding down. Their individual profiles can be summarized like this:

Profile of Jerry
Age 46

Strengths	Weaknesses
1. Skilled talker, communicator	1. Impatient listener
2. Outgoing, friendly	2. Sometimes superficial
3. Persistent, determined	3. Conniving
4. Disciplined	4. Rigid, critical
5. Courageous	5. Reckless, impulsive
6. Skilled, thorough	6. Picky, demanding

Profile of Alice
Age 41

Strengths	Weaknesses
1. Excellent listener	1. Quiet, withdrawn
2. Compassionate	2. Overly sentimental
3. Perceptive about people	3. People-pleaser
4. Sensitive	4. Easily hurt
5. Accepting of others	5. Lenient
6. Loyal, dedicated	6. Possessive

When looking at Jerry and Alice's strengths and weaknesses, you'll notice two things: 1) strengths often have a weak side; and 2) opposites often attract. Years earlier, during their courtship, Jerry and Alice fell in love with the person whose strengths complemented their weaknesses. Within a short time, appreciation for the strengths of their mate was replaced by irritation with their weaknesses. As a result, the unappreciated strengths diminished. "Why can't you be more like me?" was more than an occasional comment; it was acted out in the frustration of every day. A struggle began as each attempted to change the other.

To complicate matters further, they had two children, fifteen-year-old Shawna, and eleven-year-old Taylor. Shawna was the free spirit with an outgoing, friendly personality. She made friends easily and loved to hang out with them. Life was a lark, and she was the free-flying bird. She was critical of her dad's perfectionism and became infuriated when he said, "If you'd develop some discipline in your life, you could amount to something."

Taylor was a different combo. With technical skills, he loved tinkering with a computer, phone, or game. He could surf the internet for hours while life floated by. Taylor grew sullen when Dad said, "Taylor, why don't you make friends like Shawna does? If you were friendlier, you'd have lots of friends." Shawna's school grades were below average (and well below her ability) while Taylor's grades were excellent.

Jerry and Alice's lack of appreciation for each other translated into sharp differences over how to raise Shawna and Taylor. Jerry rode Shawna and Taylor to shape up while Alice did the opposite. Alice's leniency with Shawna and Taylor irritated Jerry. He felt undermined when she said, within earshot of both kids, "Jerry, just lighten up on Shawna and Taylor. You're always coming down on them." Life became a daily battle—attempting to change one another and refusing to change themselves.

PRESSURE AND RESISTANCE TO CHANGE

Stated as a general principle that Murphy (of the infamous "Murphy's Law") would approve: the more you attempt to change someone, the more they resist change. The pressure to change produces an equal or greater resistance to change. The greater the driving forces to change, the greater the resistance to change.

Picture this scene: a husband drops his clothes on the floor each night to the aggravation of his meticulous wife. Watch the driving and resistance forces in this exchange.

Wife: "Would you please hang up your clothes so I don't have to walk over them or iron them again?"

Husband: "Whatever." (He's heard this before.)

[Nothing changes. He continues to drop his clothes on the floor.]

Wife: "Honey, I told you to pick up your clothes so I don't have to pick them up. I'm not your mother, you know."

Husband: "They're my clothes, so don't get uptight. I earned the money to buy them, and it doesn't hurt if they're on the floor."

Wife: "They may be your clothes, but I have to wash and iron them."

Husband: "Fine. Don't wash and iron them. I'll take them to the cleaners."

Wife: "Take them to the cleaners? We can't afford that!"

Husband: "Well, with the way my shirt looked after you ironed it last time, I should have left it on the floor."

Wife: "What? If I didn't spend all my time picking up after you, I'd have more time to do a careful job of ironing."

[Since words are not succeeding, she devises a clever plan: she hides clothes left on the floor. One morning, he notices his closet is depleted.]

Husband: "Where did all my slacks and shirts go? I'm missing socks too."

Wife: "Well, have you been picking them up? When I was growing up if I didn't pick up my clothes, my mother put them away until I learned to pick them up."

Husband: "I didn't marry your mother. Don't you ever pull that again. I'll leave my clothes any place I like."

I repeat the principle: *The greater the pressure to change, the greater the resistance to change.* The result? A stubborn standoff, with hostility in the relationship. "Hardheadedness" makes for "hardheartedness," which makes for a "hard life." The Scripture says, "A tenderhearted person lives a blessed life; a hardhearted person lives a hard life" (Prov. 28:14 MSG). Or to put it another way, "the stubborn are headed for serious trouble" (NLT). The affection that was once in the relationship has turned sour; the love cord is kinked. The pressure to change simmers under the surface, with occasional explosions. Home becomes an emotional, toxic dumpsite, brimming with anger and resentment. Without a resolution, separation or divorce may seem to be the only solution.

Put this book down for a minute and align the tips of your fingers and thumb on your left hand with the tips of the fingers and thumb on your right hand. Push them hard against each other. Can your right hand over-power your left hand or vice versa? Maybe, but generally the force of one equals the resistance of the other. Now, release the pressure and allow your left and right fingers and thumbs to slide past each other forming a clasped hand, a oneness of left and right hand. This strong bond illustrates oneness.

The fingers and thumbs on your left and right hand are what I call "identical opposites." They're uniquely different—virtual opposites—but uniquely similar and clearly designed for each other. There are many things you can't do without using both hands. They're intended to work together though often performing opposite functions. Try opening a jar, driving a nail, or buttoning your shirt with one hand—rather difficult. I've often met with two people in a standoff, pressuring the other to change, somewhat like the right hand saying to the left hand, "When will you figure it out? You're designed backwards. Why don't you change and get it right, like me?"

What is the solution? Stop trying to fix each other. When the pressure to change is removed, the resistance to change begins to diminish. Ask forgiveness for nagging, pressuring, manipulating, resisting, pouting, etc. Begin to accept one another—after all, God designed each of us with unique differences, weaknesses, and complementary gifts. When this happens, the bond in the relationship becomes like the two hands, tightly connected but also working harmoniously to perform what couldn't be done separately. When husband and wife accept their God-designed differences and accept one another as their "identical opposite," their differences become essential components in their oneness.

Why don't you give a compliment to your complement right now?

DAY TWO—CHAPTER SIX

TIME OUT

Power Thoughts for Your Time Alone With God

The pressure to change produces an equal or greater resistance to change.

◊ How have you seen the above statement to be true in your relationships?

◊ Read James 3:13–18. What are the characteristics of the world's wisdom and God's wisdom? Write them down.

1. The world's wisdom is characterized by …

2. God's wisdom is characterized by …

◊ Ask God for wisdom to guide your life.

HOW GOD CHANGES PEOPLE

How has it worked when you set out to change someone? It's back fired when I've tried it. What brings about change? Do I have a part in the process? Here are key principles to follow in allowing God to change others as you cooperate with the process.

FIRST, GOD CHANGES PEOPLE, AND I'M NOT GOD.

God changes people on his schedule, not mine. God changes people in his way, not mine. My role is to surrender the process to God and allow him to do his work in his time. Ecclesiastes 3:11 says, "God has made everything beautiful in its own time" (NLT). God coordinates the process and the schedule.

Stop thinking, *I'll get them straightened out if you help me, Lord.* Instead, surrender the process to God. Apply "power in weakness"—a lifestyle of surrender. From personal experience, when I've attempted to change someone, the results have been at best disappointing and at worst disastrous. They may change for a short time to get me off their back, only to revert to their old behavior. In the end, they resent me for playing God in their life.

If you're under the assumption that it's your responsibility to change someone, I have disconcerting news for you: you're setting yourself up for disappointment. Surrender to God any tendency to manipulate, nag, control, or use gimmicks. The resentment produced by these human tactics usually boomerangs. Take the "I'm out to change you" badge off your shirt.

SECOND, KNOW YOUR RESPONSIBILITY—WHERE IT BEGINS AND WHERE IT ENDS.

If you're a parent, employer, or supervisor, you have an important role to correct and discipline when needed. Even with this responsibility, it's still God who does the changing.

When the relationship is a friend, spouse, co-worker, team member, etc., you have a responsibility to speak the truth in love and exhort at the appropriate time. This isn't an excuse to be passive; it simply recognizes that God is the CEO of the "change department."

Where do I begin? What is top priority? Begin with yourself; be open regarding your weaknesses and active in identifying your weaknesses and allowing God to turn them into strengths. You can really take responsibility for just one person, and that's you. My hunch is that, if you're at all like me, you have your hands full taking care of your own weaknesses.

THIRD, CHOOSE TO COOPERATE WITH GOD, USING THE ABC'S.

Here are the big three: Accept them with unconditional love; Believe in God's power and their potential; Communicate the truth in love. These three steps allow God to work the process of transformation in someone's life, and they also allow you to be a participant, being used by God but without manipulating or nagging. Throughout each step, pray, pray, and pray some more. In particular, pray for yourself. Pray you'll stay surrendered. Pray you'll not grow impatient. Pray you won't mess things up. Ask God to give you grace.

ACCEPT
THEM WITH UNCONDITIONAL LOVE

Love is patient, love is kind.
—1 Cor. 13:4

What's the meaning of love? Love is a dangerously misused word; we use it for all kinds of things. We love ice cream, we love our dog or cat, we love a singer we've never met, we love our car or stereo system, and we use the same word to express the lifetime commitment to the one we care about more than anyone else in the world. If you look up love in the twenty-two-volume print edition of *World Book Encyclopedia*, you won't find even one article on love. It simply says, "See sex, emotions."

We think of love as something that happens on some "enchanted evening" across a crowded room. Is the love still there on some "exhausted evening" when the two-year-old is sick for the third time this month, you've been laid off from your job, the electricity is about to be turned off, the washing machine quit, and the stack of unpaid bills seems higher than your wedding cake? You can feel the edginess in the air and in the words that are spoken. It will take more than euphoric feelings from some enchanted evening to make it through some exhausted evening.

What does it mean when someone says, "I love you"? Girls (and guys too) are often swept off their feet when they hear these words. Before falling off the love cliff, I recommend asking for clarification: "Thank you. I deeply appreciate your expression of love. To help me understand, what type of love are you referring to, Type A, B, F, or S?" The Greeks wisely distinguished different types of love by using four different words.

TYPE B: BIOLOGICAL LOVE

Key question: *"When you say you love me, do you mean the type of love you have for your sister or your grandma?"*

The Greeks used the word *storge* or *stergein* to describe this love. This is family love, the natural love of parents for their children, children for their parents, grandparents for their grandchildren, love of a husband and wife since they are one flesh, and a healthy and appropriate love between brothers and sisters. This is a love that's based in one's own nature, biologically rooted from shared genetics. It's non-sexual. A parent may be steaming mad with their child, and five minutes later feel overwhelming compassion and love for that same child. Brothers and sisters may fight incessantly … yet ready to defend their sibling against anyone who'd attack them. Fighting adolescent siblings often become the deepest of friends as adults. This word stergein is used in a negative sense meaning *unloving* or *without natural affection* in Romans 1:31 and 2 Timothy 3:3.

TYPE F: FRIENDSHIP LOVE

Key question: *"When you say you love me, do you mean you like me as a friend, a buddy, someone you enjoy hanging out with?"*

The Greeks used the word *philein* or *philos* to describe shared friendship between two people. The word in its various forms is used forty-five times in the New Testament. Philadelphia (which means "city of brotherly love") derives its name from this word. Friendship love is rooted in a pleasurable glow of the heart, kindled by genuine affection, fondness, and liking.[44] Whether it's a person or an object, it's pleasure-producing. In a non-relational sense, when you say, "I love my car" or "I love ice cream," this is "Type F" love—the object produces a warm glow of liking. When the object no longer gives you a pleasurable feeling, the love of liking ends.

In a relationship, philos is a "you like me" and "I like you" pleasurable attraction. Yes, there are fair-weather friendships, but don't underestimate the power of non-erotic devoted friendships that run deep and weather many storms. As Proverbs says, "A friend loves at all times, and a brother is born for adversity"

44. Kenneth S. Wuest, *Bypaths in the Greek New Testament* (Grand Rapids, MI: Wm. B. Eerdmans Publishing Co., 1940), 109–110.

(17:17), and "Faithful are the wounds of a friend, but deceitful are the kisses of an enemy" (27:6).

Friendship love may be accompanied by appropriate physical touch—the "holy kiss" (*philema*) was a non-erotic gesture of Christian love. As a believer, it's natural to have a love for your brothers and sisters in Christ—you're born again into the same family. Romans 12:10 combines Type B-Biological Love with Type F-Friendship Love: "Be devoted [Grk.word *philostorgos*, combined word of friendship love and biological love] to one another in brotherly love [Grk. word *philadelphias*, friendship love]; give preference to one another in honor" (definitions supplied).

The true-life story of Gayle Sayers and Brian Piccolo, featured in the outstanding movie *Brian's Song*, is a classic on friendship that moved me to tears.

Gayle Sayers and Brian Piccolo, star running backs for the Chicago Bears, created a sensation as the first black and white men in professional football to room together.

Reporters asked them about it. Reporter: "Do you mind living with him?" Piccolo: "Not if he doesn't use the bathroom." Reporter: "What do you two fellows talk about?" Sayers: "Oh, just the usual racist talk." They kidded each other a lot, but there was deep affection between them.

Then Piccolo contracted cancer and began to spend more time in the hospital than on the football field. The two had planned to go with their wives to the Professional Football Writers Association banquet in New York, where Sayers was to be presented the George S. Halas Award as that year's most courageous player. But the advance of the disease rendered Piccolo unable to go.

When the moment came for Sayers to receive the award, he stepped to the microphone and with tears rolling down his cheeks, unashamedly said, "You flatter me by giving me this award. But I accept it for Brian Piccolo. Brian is the man who should receive the award. I love Brian, and I'd like you to love him, too."[45]

TYPE S: SEXUAL LOVE

Key question: *"When you say you love me, do you mean you find me sexually attractive, I turn you on, and you'd like to make love to me?"*

This is erotic passion, exhilarating excitement, on-fire emotions. By God's design, sexual love is "satisfaction seeking." The Greeks used the word *eros* to describe sexual love. We get our word "erotic" from it. Eros is not intrinsically evil. Erotic love is a marvelous gift from God, but it can be twisted and perverted. Sexual passion is a selfish, empty act without the other types of love.

Sexual love is *passion-based*; biological love is parent-based; friendship love is *pleasure-based*; and the next type of love, agape love, is *prizing-based*.

TYPE A: AGAPĒ LOVE

Key question: *"When you say you love me, are you saying you value me as a person, you accept me with my faults and flaws, you want the very best for me in every situation, and you love me so deeply, you'll wait to physically consummate our love until we're married?"*

While I direct this question to relational attraction between a male and female, agapē love also applies to non-sexual relationships. This is the highest expression of love, the pinnacle, the summit. The Greeks used the word agapao in describing this type of love. This is the most frequent word for love in the New

---

45. Bruce W. Thielemann, "Gayle Sayers and Brian Piccolo: Crossing Racial Lines," *Preaching Today*, Tuesday, May 16, 2000, Tape No. 40.

Testament, appearing over 300 times in its various forms. This is highly unusual because the Greek poets and philosophers rarely used the word agapē. What is agapē love?

AGAPĒ IS GOD.

John used three words to define agapē: God is love (1 John 4:16), or God is agapē. The reverse is true as well: Agapē is God. He is the source, the giver of love. Agapē is sacrificial love, total giving, love that knows no end. Christ displayed this love on the cross in his voluntary death for sin. "Love each other in the same way I have loved you. There is no greater love than to lay down one's life for one's friends" (John 15:12-13 NLT).

AGAPĒ IS A LOVE OF PRIZING.

Friendship love is based on a pleasurable, reciprocal relationship between two people; agapē love is based on prizing or valuing someone. Agapē "speaks of a love which is awakened by a sense of value in an object which causes one to prize it."[46] God offers this love to us, even when we're unlovable. He's in the salvaging business. He loves the discarded, the shamed, the bruised, the hurting. When friendship has long been discarded due to violations in the relationships, agapē reaches out, placing value on the unlovable. "God is so rich in mercy, and he loved us so much, that even though we were dead because of our sins, he gave us life when he raised Christ from the dead. (It is only by God's grace that you have been saved!)" (Eph. 2:4–5 NLT).

AGAPĒ IS UNCONDITIONAL LOVE.

What does this mean? It means I love you … no matter what. Unconditional love removes the "ifs." It is not agapē love when you say, "I love you *if* you don't disappoint me. I love you *if* you

---

46. Kenneth S. Wuest, *Golden Nuggets from the Greek New Testament* (Grand Rapids, MI: Wm. B. Eerdmans Publishing Co., 1940), 60.

change your behavior. I love you *if* you don't hurt me. I love you *if* I continue to have feelings for you." Agapē or unconditional love includes these characteristics.

◊ Agapē love doesn't condone sin.

◊ Agapē love isn't the "silent treatment," an unspoken critical attitude.

◊ Agapē love is the power of Christ, accepting the other person as Christ accepted you.

◊ Agapē love is a choice, not a feeling.

◊ Agapē love places a high value on the person.

◊ Agapē love sees the positive potential in a glaring flaw.

◊ Agapē love accepts the total person—strengths and weaknesses.

◊ Agapē love is God's method to change a life.

AGAPĒ LOVE SEEKS THE ULTIMATE BEST FOR THE PERSON.

Sometimes the very best for the one you love is painful and extremely difficult. Agapē love doesn't mean the other person has the right to walk all over you. Agapē love doesn't accept sin as inconsequential. If your business partner is stealing funds from your company; if your adult child is doing drugs and stealing money; if someone is spreading lies about you, agape love confronts the wrong. If a spouse is having an affair and refuses to end the relationship, is the wounded spouse supposed to say, "Well, that's okay. Maybe someday you'll give up that other person because I love you so much"? No!

Recently a husband came to see me. He acknowledged having an affair. I asked his wife to join us for subsequent sessions, where it became apparent the husband didn't really want help ending the relationship with the other woman. He was more interested in having me say it was acceptable and his wife should get used to it. I explained that, before God, there was no justification for his affair, and there were severe consequences for continuing. I insisted that if he was serious about doing what God required of him, he'd change his cell phone number immediately and end the relationship. I explained the consequences that would live on for years to come when their children discovered the sad news. He had to make a choice, since marriage requires being mutually exclusive for each other. In our final session, weeping and sobbing, his wife shared her heart with him: "I love you and care very deeply for you. Even if you continue in your relationship with her, my concern for you will live on. However, we're married, and you *must* make a choice between her and me. I ache for you over the consequences you'll bring on yourself, on our children, and on your long-term peace of mind and relationship with God. Please know I love you, and this is one of the hardest things I've ever done." Sadly, he left to go with the other woman. His wife didn't stop praying for him, but she also took steps to move on with her life. This is the tough side of agape love. "Love is as strong as death, its jealousy as enduring as the grave. Love flashes like fire, the brightest kind of flame. Many waters cannot quench love, nor can rivers drown it. If a man tried to buy love with all his wealth, his offer would be utterly scorned" (Song of Songs 8:6–7 NLT).

Love endures, even when trampled on, long after feelings have vanished.

I wish it were otherwise, but there are no guarantees that someone will change. God allows human beings to make their own choices. Some people resist God, and though God could force them to change, he chooses not to. God says, "I am letting them go their blind and stubborn way, living according to their own desires" (Ps. 81:12 TLB). Jeremiah, the weeping prophet, said, "If you still refuse to listen, I will weep alone because of your pride. My eyes will overflow with tears …" (Jer. 13:17 NLT). When your heart is broken for someone, know God weeps with you.

AGAPĒ LOVE ACCEPTS THE PERSON, STRENGTHS AND WEAKNESSES, FAULTS AND FLAWS.

Last summer, I led a group of men in a study and discussion on what it means to love your wife. We memorized one verse: "Husbands, love your wives" (Eph. 5:25). Then week after week, we unwrapped what this verse means. Ask some men if they love their wives, and they say, "Sure. We made love two weeks ago." Loving your wife is so much more. It's a matter of laying your life down for her deepest needs. It's self-sacrifice. Love may be doing your dishes rather than leaving them in the sink, picking up your pile of stuff that makes her so upset. I'm convinced if a careful search of police records were completed, it would show no husband has ever been shot while mopping the floor.

AGAPĒ LOVE DISPLAYS THE CHARACTER OF GOD.

Dana Curry and Heather Mercer were held captive by the Taliban in Afghanistan. When released, they were asked, "What was the most difficult thing in your Afghan experience?" They said, "It was learning to live with six women in a very small room. We had to learn to forgive each other a lot." Forgiveness is among the identifiable characteristics of agape love in 1 Corinthians 13.

1. **Love is patient** with the faults of others (accepting them and trusting God to bring about change in his time).

2. **Love is kind** (gracious, thoughtful, and sensitive to build up rather than tear down).

3. **Love is not envious** (undercutting, spiteful, jealous).

4. **Love is not boastful** (self-centered, pushy to get its own way).

5. **Love is not proud** (not displaying an independent, stubborn spirit, resisting advice, refusing to acknowledge wrongs and ask forgiveness).

6. **Love is not rude** (not insensitive, irritable, touchy, making a scene).

7. **Love is not self-seeking** (instead, it is flexible, gentle, easy to work with, not demanding its own way).

8. **Love is not easily angered** (popping off, easily provoked, hot-headed).

9. **Love keeps no record of wrongs** (doesn't hold a grudge or bring up the past but chooses to forgive).

10. **Love does not delight in evil** (divisive, spreading gossip, taking revenge, practicing deceit) but rejoices with the truth.

11. **Love always protects the reputation of others** (seeking to give a good report, remaining loyal, and guarding confidential information).

12. **Love always trusts** (believing what God can do).

13. **Love always hopes** (anticipating what God will do).

14. **Love always perseveres** (enduring despite hardships and misunderstandings).

15. **Love never fails** (never giving up or falling away).

Great friendships are rich with agapē love and commitment. There's no finer example of agapē love in friendship than the relationship between David and Jonathan. "After David had finished talking with Saul, he met Jonathan, the king's son. There was an immediate bond of love between them, and they became the best of friends. ... And Jonathan made a solemn pact with David, because he loved him as he loved himself. Jonathan sealed the pact by taking off his robe and giving it to David, together with his tunic, sword, bow, and belt" (1 Sam. 18:1, 3–4 NLT).

Jonathan's commitment to David is astounding since David stood in the way of Jonathan's right to become king. Jonathan's entire career was in jeopardy due to his commitment to support David. Note: absolutely nothing indicates there was a sexual relationship between these two men. Those who try to read this into the account twist and distort the Scripture.

Four-Dimensional Love

Since God intended sexual love exclusively for the marital union of a man and a woman, marriage alone offers four-dimensional love. In a Spirit-filled marriage, agapē love includes the other three types of love: sexual, biological, and friendship. Biological love is the bond of oneness—"bone of my bones, flesh of my flesh" (Gen. 2:23). Friendship love is the pleasure of companionship, sexual love is the intimacy of passion, and agapē love is valuing each other as a priceless treasure. Four-dimensional love is God's ultimate for a human relationship.

DAY THREE—CHAPTER SIX

TIME OUT

Power Thoughts for Your Time Alone With God

Agapē love accepts the total person, strengths and weaknesses.

◊ What is the most difficult relationship you have faced in applying the quote above?

◊ Read Romans 15:1–7, 13.

◊ In what ways did Christ accept you as a person? If you accept the person you identified in the opening question, what will this mean in practical ways as you accept them as Christ accepted you? Write down specific ways to do this.

BELIEVE
IN WHAT GOD WILL DO

Love believes all things.
—1 Cor. 13:7

How often have you heard someone say, "Just believe in yourself"? I tried believing in myself. What a mess and disappointment! Proverbs 28:26 says bluntly, "Those who trust in themselves are foolish" (Prov. 28:26 NCV). God never tells you to believe in yourself.

You may have heard someone with a track record of failure say, "No one believes in me. How can I believe in myself when no one else supports me? Will you believe in me?" I hear their heart cry, but rather than setting them up for more failure, I respond, "God has a better plan for you than believing in yourself or having others believe in you. That's a formula for failure. I do believe in your incredible God-surrendered potential. Let's ask him to take over." And in your own self-talk, don't put your trust in yourself. Instead, remind yourself, *I believe in what God will do with my potential as I am surrendered to him.*

The love chapter, 1 Corinthians 13, says, Love "believes all things." What does this mean? "Believing all things" is not swallowing someone's lies and deceit, or ignoring their self-destructive lifestyle, or overlooking how others are being hurt and destroyed. "Believing all things" doesn't expect them to change themselves. "Believing all things" is faith and trust in God, with anticipation for what he will do. Where to begin?

BE A FRIEND.

In turning weaknesses into strengths, the friendship role is the best. "A friend loves at all times, and a brother is born for

250

adversity" (Prov. 17:17). Friends are those you can talk things over with and who will listen to you. They like you no matter what. They're willing to hear you out without always trying to fix you or fix the problem. They accept you. Friendship is a relationship built on trust and confidence. Henry David Thoreau said, "The most I can do for my friend is simply be his friend."

APPRECIATE THEIR WORTH AND VALUE.

The word "appreciate" means to "be thankful for, to express and recognize the worth and value of someone or something." If your home appreciates, the value goes up; if your car depreciates, the value goes down. The value of an appreciated person goes up; the value of a depreciated person goes down. The Scripture is clear: "Encourage one another day after day, as long as it is *still* called "Today," so that none of you will be hardened by the deceitfulness of sin" (Heb. 3:13). Did you spot the "frequency factor" for giving encouragement? Once a year on Thanksgiving? On their birthday? Once a month, once a week? No. *Daily!* The heart of a discouraged person begins to harden, and sin dances at the door. With a simple word of encouragement, you can have an enormous impact, helping the discouraged person conquer temptation and live victoriously. Who are you going to encourage today?

Let's assume your wife or mother enjoys cooking and spends hours putting her special touch on every meal with the family— elaborate garnishes, sauces, multiple courses, specialty desserts. She could be a contestant on the cooking channel. Year after year, the family sits down and prays, "Dear Lord, we thank you for this wonderful meal. Amen." The family eats without a comment about the food. Just silence, year after year after year. What's wrong with this picture? It's good they thank God for the food, but how about thanking Mom? The family never says the food is terrible. They just say nothing—stone silence.

Why? Maybe they think, *If we tell Mom she's a great cook, she'll become proud*. Nonsense! "Better is open rebuke than love that is concealed" (Prov. 27:5).

What eventually happens? Mom concludes that cooking really doesn't matter since no one appreciates it. She digs the leftovers out of the refrigerator, plops them on a plate, and microwaves them. Leftovers are served so often, the family wonders if she's borrowing them from the neighbors. When she doesn't want to cook, she hollers, "There's a TV dinner in the freezer. *Bon appétit*." What? It's more like "gone appetite." What you fail to appreciate will diminish and disappear.

Write down genuine affirmation you can give to those closest to you. Now look for the right time and setting to communicate your words. When the person you're speaking to recovers from the shock, repeat it. I'm not suggesting this be done in a mechanical way or insincere manner. For your grown and married children, you may want to write an affirming letter, something like this:

Bill, we appreciate you as a son-in-law. You came into the life of our daughter with tenderness, caring, and spiritual leadership. We know this was God's doing. Thank you for being a fine husband, father, businessman, provider, and a man of God.

Susie, you're our daughter and always will be. You're such a beauty, a gem, a treasure, and we're thrilled to be Dad and Mom to you. So often you encourage us with your thoughtful words. You're a great wife, mother, and second-grade teacher. You're a person of spiritual maturity and love. We're exceptionally proud of you.

Bill and Susie, we bless you both and treasure you, and pray God's greatest blessing on your home and your lives. All we can say is, "We love you both!"

Don't stick a jab in your note of affirmation: "Bill and Susie, we hope and pray you'll start having family devotions," or "We hope you get your car loan paid off soon." This will negate the entire affirmation.

Nicknames may also be used to affirm but choose carefully since nicknames may be derogatory as well as complimentary. When you give someone a nickname, make certain it's a name they're comfortable with. Calling a son "Tiger" or a daughter "Princess" can affirm them as a person and affect how they see themselves. I gave Joanne's parents, Henry and Elizabeth, royalty nicknames: "King Henry and Queen Elizabeth." This caught on with some of the family, and it was fun to see them light up when we called them King or Queen.

IDENTIFY THEIR POTENTIAL.

Let's return to the home of Jerry, Alice, Shawna, and Taylor, where criticism has been thick in the air. What can be done to break through the ill feelings they have for each other? Here's a starting point:

Jerry to his wife: "Alice, I'm sorry for trying to change you. You're God's special person, uniquely designed to be who you are. You're great with people, so sensitive and accepting. I admire how you make people feel loved and accepted. Thanks for being such a great listener."

Alice to her husband: "Jerry, it makes me blush when you say this, but it also makes me feel valued and appreciated. Thank you. When something needs to get done and done right, you're the man. Thanks for your hard work in providing for the family. I admire and respect you for not quitting when things get tough."

The husband needs respect and affirmation; the wife needs approval and love. If they fail in supporting one another with these positives, they'll drag each other down with their negatives, as columnist Janie B. Cheaney observed in WORLD magazine: "If men and women don't mutually pledge their strengths, they will default to their weaknesses. The harder a woman pushes, the faster a man retreats. The more a man forfeits, the more a woman takes on. He gets lazy, she gets bitter. He turns violent, she becomes passive."[47]

Jerry and Alice also have the opportunity to extend this attitude to Shawna and Taylor, affirming their worth and identifying potential.

Jerry to his daughter: "Shawna, you're great with people, with your warm smile, bubbly personality, and ability to communicate. Have you ever thought about going into public relations? Some company will be thrilled to hire you. You might even make a great television news reporter. Whatever, you will do well as you follow God in your life. I'm so proud of you."

Alice to her son: "Taylor, you're so great with computers. I'm just lost with these technical things, and you're an absolute genius. I'm so blessed to have a son like you. Who knows? You may be designing the computer chip for the next trip to outer space someday."

No matter how buried or camouflaged, every person has undeveloped potential. You're in a unique position to help others by identifying their potential. What do you see in their life that they're not aware of but need encouragement in developing? Study the person, asking God in prayer, "Lord, what is _____'s undeveloped potential, and how can I encourage them in it?" In identifying potential, you're not determining God's will for their life; you're simply helping them become aware of possibilities.

Years ago, I was emotionally locked up and carrying unresolved issues, but Joanne saw in me what I didn't see. I remember her saying, "You have a remarkable caring and kindness that I don't think you realize." I was surprised by her words, and she wasn't conning me. She saw in me what I didn't see and today that's

---

47. Janie B. Cheaney, "Male call," *World Magazine*, September 5, 2011, 20.

who I am. Be a person who believes and anticipates what God will do.

What about telling someone you're proud of them? Many Christians are uncomfortable using the word "proud" as a word of affirmation. Being prideful is sin, and many of the biblical uses of the word "pride" do refer to sin. However, the same Greek word is used to describe bad as well as good pride. For example, Paul writes to the Corinthians, "Great is my confidence in you; great is my boasting on your behalf" (2 Cor. 7:4), and again he says, "Therefore openly before the churches, show them the proof of your love and of our reason for boasting about you" (2 Cor. 8:24). Writing to the Galatians, Paul says, "Each one must examine his own work, and then he will have reason for boasting in regard to himself alone, and not in regard to another" (Gal. 6:4). As Joseph Thayer suggests, the pride condemned in the Bible is "an insolent and empty assurance which trusts in its own power and resources and shamefully despises and violates divine laws and human laws."[48] On the other hand, when pride is approved in the Bible, it is giving glory to God for what he is doing in a person's life. They are commended for being a surrendered vessel allowing God to work. For example, one couple, both of whom were relatively new Christians, were going through a terrible time of suffering. I said to them, "I am proud of you both for standing strong in your faith." In this sense, it is appropriate to say, "I'm proud of you."

---

48. Thayer, *Greek-English Lexicon of the New Testament*, 25.

DAY FOUR—CHAPTER SIX

TIME OUT
Power Thoughts for Your Time Alone With God

The value of an appreciated person goes up.

◊ When you receive an appreciative comment from someone, what impact does that have on you, immediately and in future actions?

◊ Read Hebrews 3:12–14 and 10:24–25. Why do you think discouragement can be a set-up to fall into temptation?

◊ When is the last time you encouraged someone? What steps will you take to encourage someone today?

COMMUNICATE
TRUTHFULLY IN A LOVING MANNER

Love is patient, love is kind.
—1 Cor. 13:4

God can greatly use a word spoken in the right circumstance. Here are principles to communicate in a way that God will use.

SPEAK THE TRUTH IN LOVE.

Truth and love are the perfect balance in communication. "Do not let kindness and truth leave you; bind them around your neck, write them on the tablet of your heart" (Prov. 3:3–5). If they're around your neck and on your heart, they're with you all the time. Learn balance in your communication. Not every truthful word is kind, and not every kind word is truthful. Paul said, "Speak the truth in love, growing in every way more and more like Christ" (Eph. 4:15 NLT). Growing in Christ-likeness is learning to speak truthfully in love.

How is this applied? When your husband walks in from work and says, "Why's this place always a pigsty when I get home from work?" he sets the tone for a hostile, tense evening. He may have spoken truthfully but certainly not kindly. Instead, if this is an important issue, he should discuss it in a truthful and loving manner, at the right time. "I really value things picked up at home, as it helps me relax and unwind. How could we work together to make this possible?"

While our two daughters were growing up, eating noises were a touchy issue. Without giving away identities, two of us were "munchers," and two were "glarers." Here's how it worked: munchers chewed carrots, granola, apples, celery, or gum with mouth partially open for increased effect, carefully chewing

258

each bite hundreds of times (or so it seemed) to aid digestion. Effectively practiced, it prompted irritated, angry glares. Glarers metaphorically threw deadly daggers across the room without speaking a word. What a crazy issue! After numerous blow-ups, I decided to employ all my skills of international diplomacy. I convinced the glarers to stop stomping out of the room and the munchers to do their crunching in the kitchen. Speaking the truth in love meant saying something like this: "You know, your munching of the carrots is irritating. If you could chew them in the kitchen, I'll look forward to having you rejoin me later."

INVITE CONSTRUCTIVE CRITICISM.

Be open to areas where you need to grow. My wife has my invitation to give input that will help me as a person, including critiquing what I wear. One day she said, "You know, that shirt is really out of style." I replied, "Hon, I don't follow the fashions. I set the styles." She shot right back, "Strange that none of those styles have caught on."

Seriously, do yourself a big favor by having someone give you helpful input. "If you profit from constructive criticism, you will be elected to the wise men's hall of fame. But to reject criticism is to harm yourself and your own best interest" (Prov. 15:32 TLB).

SHARE CONSTRUCTIVE CRITICISM IN PRIVATE.

Is your friend or spouse sensitive or self-conscious about his or her weaknesses? Most of us are. Public embarrassment or ridicule of the other person's fault or idiosyncrasy will inflame bitter resentment. One husband brought up the subject of his wife being overweight in a joking but cutting manner at nearly every party they attended. He couldn't understand why she continued to gain weight.

Bob Thune and I met for the first time the night we prayed to receive Christ. He was seven, and I was six years old. Little did we know that years later we'd be college roommates and be in each other's wedding—one day apart. During high school, we met each morning in the basement of his home to pray before going to band practice. Our burden was to share Christ with every guy in our high school. The Lord opened opportunities to do this and several came to know Christ. Bob excelled at nearly everything; he was an all-state athlete in football, basketball, and track, and an honor student. I was first-team mediocre in sports and had "by the grace of God" grades. In band, we both played trumpet. I challenged him for first chair and beat him, which meant I sat in front of him. To spite me, he enjoyed filling his trumpet slide with water and dumping it on my head.

One morning, I retaliated. While Bob and I were piously praying in the basement of his home, I arranged for his brother, Rich, to remove his trumpet from the case, fill it with frilly underwear, and pack it as tightly as possible. When Bob arrived in band, he flipped the case open and underwear flew out. He was furious and stomped from the room. To retaliate, he put a firecracker in my back pocket, lit it, and enjoyed my reaction to the explosion. (Don't try this. Serious injury could occur.)

Bob and I had a strange and wonderful relationship. He was wonderful, and I was strange. I was uncouth and socially inept, and Bob frequently corrected me. With my insecurities, I was defensive. After his senior year, Bob left for Biola on an athletic scholarship, while I completed my last year of high school in our hometown of Murdo, South Dakota. Toward the end of my senior year, he called me from California and said, "Dave, I want you to come to Biola and be my roommate." I was surprised and nervous about the invite—did I want to be open to further correction? However, I sensed he really wanted to be with me, and I accepted his offer. Rooming together for four years was life-changing for me. Bob continued to correct me which I needed but with a loving spirit, and I grew to be less defensive. Further, I asked Bob for constructive criticism knowing he had my best interests at heart. Bob would often say, "Dave, you have a heart for God and that is what is most important." Bob became a great encourager in my life, and he helped me identify my undeveloped potential.

Four of us roomed together in a quad during college, and these three guys—Bob Thune, Rich Thune, and Howard Parker—had an enormous impact on my life. "As iron sharpens iron, so a friend sharpens a friend" (Prov. 27:17 NLT). Years later, we're still very close. I see how those three guys practiced the ABC's: 1) They *accepted* me with agape love; 2) They *believed* in my God-surrendered potential; and 3) They *communicated* correction in a truthful, loving manner. Practice the ABC's in a relationship, and you will have a great impact on other lives.

KNOW WHEN TO DROP AN ISSUE.

Don't nag. A kitchen appliance manufacturer received the warranty card sent in by the purchaser. After the question, "What prompted you to buy this appliance?" were three words: *nag, nag, nag*. Proverbs says it's better to live in a desert or an attic than with a crabby, nagging person in a lovely home (Prov. 21:9, 19). In most cases, after clearly communicating a constructive criticism and explaining why it's important, drop it. As noted earlier, human nature is such that the very pressure to change usually produces an equal or greater resistance to that change.

GIVE UP THE MYTH OF PERFECT COMPATIBILITY.

Don't expect perfect compatibility. Don't expect a total personality makeover. It's not going to happen. Some of the quirks are the uniqueness of the person. Dr. Francis Schaeffer had a profound influence on Christianity, but his wife, Edith, saw things that irritated her like his muddy boots, being late for dinner, etc. She had to decide: either create an atmosphere of hostility in the home or choose to make the most of every day. She chose the latter. She often lit a candle for dinner and put a slice of lemon in his water and performed other kindnesses she knew he'd appreciate.

In describing his more than sixty-year marriage, Billy Graham said, "Ruth and I are happily incompatible."

When weaknesses collide, go back to the **ABC's**. **A**ccept them with unconditional love. **B**elieve in what God will do. **C**ommunicate the truth in love. These are your "loving edge" to be used by God in a relationship.

DAY FIVE—CHAPTER SIX

TIME OUT

Power Thoughts for Your Time Alone With God

If you profit from constructive criticism, you will be elected to the wise men's hall of fame. But to reject criticism is to harm yourself and your own best interest.
—Prov. 15:32 TLB

◊ Read Proverbs 27:5–17.

◊ When was the last time someone criticized you? What was your response? How could your response have been better?

◊ Identify a time when criticism was just what you needed in your life. How did it impact you to become a stronger person?

◊ Who's the sharpening person in your life?

TIME TOGETHER

SESSION SIX

FIXIN' THE WEAKNESSES IN OTHERS?

Differences can be a major source of frustration in relationships often resulting in tension and edginess when you're together. How do you handle being in the same household with an opposite who grates on your nerves? Do you keep quiet or speak up? Does it work to try to change the person? Is there a way to cooperate with God as he works to change someone? In this session, we dig for answers to these questions and more. Let's get started.

CONNECT

◊ As a group, take the "Compatibility Quiz" at the start of this chapter. Have someone read each item one at a time and then pause. Raise your hand if it applies to you and you're courageous enough to say so. Elbowing the person next to you is allowed (just don't break any ribs).

GROW

◊ Read Romans 15:1–7 as a group. Identify and share your strengths and weaknesses with the group. Do they see you this way?

◊ Discuss how to apply the ABC's in your personal relationships.

Accepting each other with unconditional love

Believing in what God will do

Communicating the truth in love

APPLY

◊ One at a time, read through the characteristics of love from 1 Corinthians 13 and discuss applying them in your relationships.

1. *Love is patient* with the faults of others (accepting them and trusting God to bring about change in his time).

2. *Love is kind* (gracious, thoughtful, and sensitive to build up rather than tear down).

3. *Love is not envious* (undercutting, spiteful, jealous).

4. *Love is not boastful* (self-centered, pushy to get its own way).

5. *Love is not proud* (not displaying an independent, stubborn spirit, resisting advice, refusing to acknowledge wrongs and ask forgiveness).

6. *Love is not rude* (not insensitive, irritable, touchy, making a scene).

7. *Love is not self-seeking* (instead, it is flexible, gentle, easy to work with, not demanding its own way).

8. *Love is not easily angered* (popping off, easily provoked, hot-headed).

9. *Love keeps no record of wrongs* (doesn't hold a grudge or bring up the past but chooses to forgive).

10. *Love does not delight in evil* (divisive, spreading gossip, taking revenge, practicing deceit) but rejoices with the truth.

11. *Love always protects the reputation* of others (seeking to give a good report, remaining loyal, and guarding confidential information).

12. *Love always trusts* (believing what God can do).

13. *Love always hopes* (anticipating what God will do).

14. *Love always perseveres* (enduring despite hardships and misunderstandings).

15. *Love never fails* (never giving up or falling away).

◊ Read aloud in unison the "Changing My Mind" verse for this week.

Accept One Another

Therefore, accept each other just as Christ has accepted you so that God will be given glory.

—Rom. 15:7 NLT

PRAY

◊ If group members are in difficult relationships, spend time supporting them in prayer. Both alone and in the group, pray for each other.

◊ With the conclusion of your six weeks together, how will you continue to keep in touch? Do you plan to do another study together?

◊ Has your group considered doing a service project together to share God's love? Painting, cleaning, pruning, repairing? If this is something the group decided to do, you may want to plan a celebration meal together after the service project is completed.

SHARE

◊ Be alert to people you meet who are exhausted, discouraged, or frustrated. Look for an opportunity to share an encouraging word of affirmation or listen to them with compassion.

◊ Here are some thought-provoking questions that may ignite a discussion this week.

1. What is love?

2. Have you ever attempted to change someone? How did it work out?

3. What does it mean to be accepted by another person?

YOUR WINNING EDGE TO THRIVE

Whoever trusts in his riches will fall,
but the righteous will thrive like the green leaf.
—Prov. 11:28

An "edge" may be the cutting side of a knife or the precipice of a dangerous cliff. An "edge" may also be intense vigor and energy—a "cutting edge" to achieve. Closely related, an "edge" may also refer to keenness and intensity of desire—a "motivational edge." Weaknesses empowered by God are your "winning edge" to overcome seemingly insurmountable obstacles.

Here are some final thoughts to hit the road of life with a "winning edge" to thrive.

FIRST, NEVER FORGET THE "EDGE OF RUIN" THAT GOD PULLED YOU FROM OR KEPT YOU FROM.

What would your life be like left to your own devices? As David said, "You pulled me from the brink of death, my feet from the cliff-edge of doom. Now I stroll at leisure with God in the sunlit fields of life" (Ps. 56:13 MSG). Acknowledge your weakness.

SECOND, BE VIGILANT NOT TO SLIP BACK TO THE "EDGE OF DISASTER."

It's easy to get careless and fall back into old patterns. Obadiah warned his contemporaries: "All your old partners will drive you to the edge. Your old friends will lie to your face. Your old drinking buddies will stab you in the back. Your world will collapse. You won't know what hit you" (Obad. 1:7 MSG). Keep the cutting-edge of your expectations sharp. Jesus said, "Be on your guard. Don't let the sharp edge of your expectation get dulled by parties and drinking and shopping" (Luke 21:34 MSG).

THIRD, RELEASE RESENTMENTS AND REGRETS.

David said, "I'm on the edge of losing it—the pain in my gut keeps burning" (Ps. 38:17 MSG). You can either live with your teeth on edge and your stomach in a knot, or you can release resentments and regrets before they get a stranglehold on you. Practice forgiveness.

FOURTH, REFUEL DAILY TO RENEW YOUR EDGE OF VIGOR AND ENERGY.

Life will take it out of you—guaranteed. God promises to energize those who get tired, and he gives fresh strength to those who wait on him (Isa. 40:29–31). Meditate daily on the Word of God, and God will give you success in your endeavors (Ps. 1). "Your commands give me an edge on my enemies; they never become obsolete" (Ps. 119:98 MSG). Refuel daily: "You're my place of quiet retreat; I wait for your Word to renew me" (Ps. 119:114 MSG).

FIFTH, REMEMBER THE SECRET OF YOUR STRENGTH.

God promises, "My power is strongest when you are weak" (1 Cor. 12:9 CEV). Make it your life motto: "When I am weak, I am strong" (2 Cor. 12:10 NLT).

POWER IN WEAKNESS!

… your "winning edge" to thrive!

Appendix A

THREE SIMPLE STEPS TO NEW LIFE

Beginning the Christian life is as simple as the ABCs backward. Today you can begin the most thrilling adventure of your life as a follower of Jesus Christ. Here's how.

Confess your sins. You may have lived a good, moral life, but the Bible says, "All have sinned and fall short of the glory of God" (Rom. 3:23), and "the wages of sin is death, but the gift of God is eternal life in Christ Jesus our Lord" (Rom. 6:23). The Bible also says, "God showed his great love for us by sending Christ to die for us while we were still sinners" (Rom. 5:8 NLT). Jesus Christ shed his blood on the cross to pay the penalty for your sins and to provide complete forgiveness. Confess your sins and ask Christ to forgive your sins. God "… is patient toward you, not wishing for any to perish but for all to come to repentance" (2 Pet. 3:9).

Believe in Jesus Christ as your Savior and Lord. When a religious man asked Jesus how to get to heaven, Jesus told him, "For God loved the world so much that he gave his one and only Son, so that everyone who believes in him will not perish but have eternal life" (John 3:16 NLT). Believing in Jesus Christ is a simple choice and a step of faith. "If you confess with your mouth that Jesus is Lord and believe in your heart that God raised him from the dead, you will be saved" (Rom. 10:9 NLT).

Accept Christ into your life. The Bible says, "To all who believed him and accepted him, he gave the right to become children of God. They are reborn—not with a physical birth resulting from human passion or plan, but a birth that comes from God" (John 1:12–13 NLT). By accepting or asking Christ into your life, he now lives within you. "This is the secret: Christ lives in you" (Col. 1:27 NLT).

Dear God,

I confess my sin. Thank you that you forgive every sin because of Christ's death on the cross.

I believe in Jesus Christ. I place my faith and trust in him. He proved himself to be God through his miraculous life, his death on the cross, and resurrection from the dead.

I accept Jesus Christ into my life. By your Spirit, I invite you to live within me.

Signed:_____

Date:_____

Appendix B

A GUIDE FOR SMALL GROUPS

The shared journey is the best journey. If you went on a cruise to Alaska or snorkeling in the Caribbean, would you rather go alone or have a friend to share the experience with? When you see something beautiful or experience something spectacular, you naturally want to tell someone about it. God designed us with a need to connect, to share our joys as well as our sorrows with someone who understands. The impact of your six-week personal growth journey will be doubled when others travel with you. Select one or two other people to share the journey with or develop a small group with several participants. Don't miss the joy of the shared journey.

WHY SMALL GROUPS?

In this world driven to achieve big results and big crowds, small groups may seem … well, small … as in insignificant and unimportant. God disagrees. The ancient prophet asked, "Who has despised the day of small things?" (Zech. 4:10). Small groups are God's idea for fellowship. You can worship with a large crowd, but you can't fellowship with five thousand people. The big crowd fosters loneliness; the small group builds friendships.

ARE SMALL GROUPS BIBLICAL?

From the earliest days of the Church, the believers met in small groups, usually in someone's home. After the conversion and baptism of 3,000 (recorded in Acts 2:38–41), they began meeting together for teaching, fellowship, prayer, and breaking of bread from house to house (Acts 2:42, 46). This was authentic Christianity at the cell level. As the Church continued to grow and persecution broke out, Acts 5:42 says, "Every day, in the temple and from house to house, they kept right on teaching and preaching Jesus as the Christ" (Acts 5:42). Before Paul became a follower of Jesus, he was ravaging the church, going house to house as they met and dragging Christians off to prison (Acts 8:3). After God got hold of his life and spun him around, Paul went from terrorizing believers house to house to teaching believers house to house (Acts 20:20). Paul also mentions a church in the house of Aquila and Priscilla (Rom. 16:3, 5; 1 Cor. 16:19), Gaius (Rom. 16:23), Philemon (Philem. 1, 2), and Nympha in Laodicea (Col. 4:15).

The intimacy of the home and the dynamic of the small group provide a natural setting for spiritual growth, but groups can meet wherever it works—a coffee shop, restaurant, at the workplace, or in a park. You name the setting, and Jesus will meet you there. A small group can be two or three people or as many as twelve to fifteen. And remember, the Lord is present whenever you meet. The presence of Jesus makes your group, large or small, an exciting place to be.

TIPS FOR LEADING A SMALL GROUP

Being a facilitator for a small group is not as difficult as it may seem. You don't have to be a preacher or even a great talker. If you're taking the lead in a small group, here are some tips.

Prepare in advance. Read the Bible passages, think through the questions, and pray for the members of the group before each session.

Don't do it all yourself. Before you begin, if possible, select a co-leader to assist you and to lead from time to time. Have someone else coordinate a refreshment schedule so everyone brings something. You may also want to rotate homes.

Introduce newcomers. Make certain everyone knows the others in the group by name. The Connect section that opens each session is designed to facilitate knowing each other personally and deepening your relationships.

Prepare a group roster. Have a group member make a list of the names, phone numbers, and email addresses of group members and distribute a copy to each person. Don't forget to update it when a new person joins the group.

Relax and be who you are. Rather than worrying about the impression you're making on others, greet each person with a warm smile. Be interested in them and enjoy laughing together. If someone asks a question you don't have an answer to, say so. You don't have to be a know-it-all. They will respect you for being a learner with them.

Ask questions and listen. Being an effective group leader is more about listening than telling. The questions included with each session are designed for discussion. If you add questions of your own, don't use closed-ended questions. These are questions that are answered with a yes or no or require no more than a one- or two-word answer. They close off a discussion. Instead, use open-ended questions. For example, instead of asking "Do you think this is important?" ask "Why do you think this is important?" Ask "How did you feel when …?" or "What would you recommend to someone facing this situation?" Don't panic if you ask a question, and there isn't an immediate response. Be patient as group members gather their thoughts.

Rotate around the group for Scripture reading. To involve everyone, have each person read one or two verses.

Affirm the responses of group members. After someone shares, show your appreciation by saying something like, "Thanks for sharing that" or "That was a helpful insight." Then for those who haven't shared, ask, "Would someone else like to add to this?" or "We haven't had the opportunity to hear from everyone on this. Who else would like to share?" Even if someone gives a wrong answer, don't put them down. Gently give another perspective. Be sensitive to those who are new or reluctant to speak up or pray out loud. Give them a safe place. As they begin to feel more comfortable, they'll come along. Don't force or pressure them.

Don't allow one or two people to dominate the discussion. If an individual is taking over the discussion, say something like, "Thank you, Joe, for sharing. And since we haven't heard from the others, let's hear what they have to offer." If it continues to be a problem, meet alone with him, where you can say something like, "Joe, I'm pleased you're part of the group, and you have good things to share. However, I want to ask you to help me help the quieter members participate equally. Please give a brief comment, and then let's pass the opportunity to others."

Break into smaller groups. If your group is larger than seven people, divide into smaller groups of two to four people for part of the session. This is also an effective setting for prayer. The quieter person will feel more comfortable praying out loud when the group is smaller. This smaller group can become a "prayer partnership." Encourage them to be in touch during the week by phone, email, or text.

Pray and worship together. Allow individuals to share their prayer concerns and then take the time to pray for each other. Encourage short prayers. Occasionally you may want the group to pray using one-sentence prayers. This can be particularly effective when praising God for his attributes and blessings. Sometimes you'll want to stand and join hands in a circle as you pray. This creates a strong sense of unity. Music can also be a vital part of prayer. If someone plays an instrument, you can ask them to lead in a simple song of praise. Or you can select a song on a Christian CD and play it as the group sings along. Make certain the song is not too difficult for singing as a group.

Go with the flow. It isn't necessary to cover all the questions. Be flexible. Make certain the meeting doesn't go too long. A good discussion can continue after the group is dismissed if this is acceptable to the host.

TIPS FOR HOSTING A SMALL GROUP

The thought of others coming to your home can be quite intimidating. If you're uptight about making a good impression, you will have difficulty enjoying the group. Instead of feeling you have to entertain your guests, choose to relax and give hospitality to your guests. Here are the crucial differences.

ENTERTAINING VERSUS HOSPITALITY

There is a world of difference between entertaining and hospitality. Entertaining seeks to impress others; hospitality seeks to be interested in others. When you're entertaining, you're constantly asking yourself, "What are they thinking? Am I making a good impression?" With hospitality, the focus is on your guest, not on yourself. Ask caring questions. Listen with love and understanding. Often, entertaining creates pressure to perform, which then creates fear and nervousness. Hospitality is different. You can tell when you're practicing hospitality because it will almost always be a joyful experience. You sense God using you to show love to others. Peter reminded the believers, "Most important of all, continue to show deep love for each other, for love covers a multitude of sins. Cheerfully share your home with those who need a meal or a place to stay" (1 Pet. 4:8–9 NLT).

WHAT IS IMPORTANT FOR YOUR GUESTS?

Think through the last time you were invited as a guest to someone's home. Check below what was essential for you to feel comfortable and welcomed. This will help you know what is really important when people come to your home.

◊ Home spotlessly clean and closets organized

◊ Silver tea service, imported cups, and saucers

◊ Feeling the host was glad you came

Your Winning Edge

◊ Windows washed, and carpets cleaned

◊ Furnishings that could be featured in *Home & Decor*

◊ The host asks how your week has been

◊ Home comfortably clean

◊ Fresh-cut flowers

◊ Gourmet entrees and expensive desserts

◊ Relaxed setting

◊ Feeling accepted as a person

◊ Healthy and tasty snacks

◊ Kick-your-shoes-off comfortable

◊ Being listened to

GROUP GUIDELINES

To keep things on track expect the group to commit to some practices that make for a healthy group. At the beginning of a new study, read through these guidelines, discuss, and agree to practice them. This may be duplicated for the group.

Stay Focused and Balanced. We meet to worship God, fellowship together, grow in the Word of God, apply the Word to our lives to serve others, and share our faith with unbelievers.

Group Attendance. To stay in touch with one another, we will call, text, or send an email if we are unable to attend or running late. This will be our goal for when the group starts and ends: Arrival time: _____ Starting time: _____ Ending time: _____These are the calendar dates we will be meeting: _____ _____

Guard Confidences. We will be careful to avoid sharing confidential information outside the group.

Healthy Group Life. We will be careful to avoid dominating the conversation, and we will always look for the opportunity for everyone to share. We will seek to make this a safe place where others can share their struggles without receiving a snap judgment or a quick fix to their problem. We will be sensitive to the special needs of group members. Some may have to leave for work at 4:30 a.m., so we will be careful not to go too late; some may have dietary restrictions so we will be alert to these when planning refreshments or a meal together, and some may be struggling with alcohol, so we recognize it is best not to serve alcoholic beverages.

Welcome Newcomers. We will look for opportunities to invite friends and warmly welcome newcomers to the group.

ASK AND YOU SHALL RECEIVE

ɔsus said, *You may ask me for anything in my name, and I will do it* (John 14:14). This was so
nportant, so strategic, that Jesus repeated it six times in his final night with his disciples before
is crucifixion (John 14:13, 14, 15:7, 16; 16:24, 26). The promise is yours today: *ask and you
hall receive.* As a group, share your prayer requests and praise reports. This is a place to write
own those requests and to make notes of answers to prayer. This may be duplicated for the
roup.

Date	Pray Request	Answer to Prayer

Dave & Joanne Beckwith

God's VIPs

Members of Your Small Group
(This may be duplicated for use in a small group)

Name and Contact Information	**Phone Contact**
Name: _____	(____) _____
Email: _____	(____) _____
Name: _____	(____) _____
Email: _____	(____) _____
Name: _____	(____) _____
Email: _____	(____) _____
Name: _____	(____) _____
Email: _____	(____) _____
Name: _____	(____) _____
Email: _____	(____) _____
Name: _____	(____) _____
Email: _____	(____) _____
Name: _____	(____) _____
Email: _____	(____) _____
Name: _____	(____) _____
Email: _____	(____) _____
Name: _____	(____) _____
Email: _____	(____) _____
Name: _____	(____) _____
Email: _____	(____) _____

Releasing Resentments

This is a walk-through of the steps to release resentments. Use this worksheet or a separate sheet of paper, which may be destroyed later. Don't overlook resentments that may be decades old. You may copy this worksheet for yourself or your small group.

Description of a Resentment (Injustice, Mistreatment, Pain, Circumstance)	Type of Resentment (1, 2, 3, 4)	Are you willing to forgive?	Placed on "God's-to-Do" list

Appendix D

Releasing Regrets

This is a walk-through of the steps to release regrets. Use this worksheet or a separate sheet of paper, which may be destroyed later. Think through regrets that linger in your mind. Be specific. You may copy this worksheet for yourself or your small group.

My Regrets Actions, attitudes, words spoken	Apology completed if needed	I agree with God's forgiveness	I am forgiven & set free

MEDITATION AND MEMORY VERSES

God's Power Pack

I can do all things through him who strengthens me.
Greater is he who is in me than he who is in the world.
I am more than a conqueror through him who loves me.
Absolutely nothing is impossible with God!
(Paraphrase: Phil. 4:13; 1 John 4:4; Rom. 8:37; Luke 1:37)

Changing My Mind – Week 1

Power Perfected in Weakness

"My grace is sufficient for you, for power is perfected in
weakness." Most gladly, therefore, I will rather boast
about my weaknesses, so that the power of Christ may
dwell in me. (2 Cor. 12:9 NASB)

Changing My Mind – Week 2

A Mental Makeover

Don't copy the behavior and customs of this world, but
let God transform you into a new person by changing the
way you think.
(Rom. 12:2 NLT)

Changing My Mind – Week 3

Weed Killer for a Bitter Root

Look after each other so that none of you fails to receive
the grace of God. Watch out that no poisonous root of
bitterness grows up to trouble you, corrupting many.
(Heb. 12:15 NLT)

Changing My Mind – Week 4

Blameless

Even before he made the world, God loved us
and chose us in Christ to be holy and
without fault in his eyes. (Eph. 1:4 NLT)

Changing My Mind – Week 5

Accept One Another

Therefore, accept each other just as Christ has accepted
you so that God will be given glory.
(Rom. 15:7 NLT)

Changing My Mind – Week 6

ABOUT THE AUTHORS
DAVE AND JOANNE BECKWITH

One week after their wedding in 1969, Dave and Joanne began their journey in pastoral ministry. And what an adventure it has been—some thrilling joys and successes along with struggles, pain, and setbacks. God has repeatedly spared Dave's life … a knife thrown at him while preaching in the Philippines, a dramatic rescue from a fiery head-on collision with a drunk driver who was driving on the wrong side of the freeway, a 40-foot fall while speaking in Northern California, and a biking accident when the driver of an SUV plowed into and ran over him. Dave relates these life lessons and many others in his speaking and teaching.

Dave's ministry experience includes youth and camp ministry, church administration, and serving as a senior pastor for over 30 years. Joanne has been an active partner in the ministry, working alongside Dave while leading women's ministries, mentoring, and teaching.

Currently, Dave and Joanne serve as shepherds with Standing Stone Ministry, caring for spiritual leaders. Dave is also the Western US Regional Director for Standing Stone, training and coordinating the work over 50 pastoral shepherds. In 2007, Dave was named senior pastor emeritus for Woodbridge Church in Irvine, California, where he served as senior pastor for nearly 20 years. He also serves as a lead pastor for churches going through transition.

Dave and Joanne are both graduates of Biola University. Joanne received her BS degree in nursing. Professionally, she has worked in alcohol and drug rehab and psychiatry. Dave received his BS degree in business administration at Biola and did his seminary work at Talbot School of Theology. Additional graduate studies have included an MA in biblical studies and PhD in church and family ministry.

A love for God's beauty in nature takes them on hikes and rides on their recumbent bikes. Their two married daughters, Julie and Tami, four grandchildren, and seven great-grandchildren are a great source of joy and enjoyment.

Having faced the painful side of personal and church life has equipped them to come alongside others. God has given them a heart for those who hurt and a shared life mission to help others discover God's power in their weakest moments. One of their greatest joys is sharing a cup of coffee or a meal—weeping with those who weep and rejoicing with those who rejoice.

You may contact them for speaking, consulting, or leader care at:

STANDING STONE MINISTRY

150 Paularino Avenue, Building B, Costa Mesa, CA 92626

dave.b@standingstoneministry.org; joanne.b@ standingstoneministry.org

www.standingstoneministry.org or www.pastorbiker.com

Scripture Index

Genesis
2:23—245
37:19-36—159
50:18-20—159

Exodus
24:18—xv

Numbers
11:1—150
11:1-6—148
11:11-15—158
11:13-15—149, 157

Deuteronomy
6:6-9—119

Joshua
1:6-9—115, 116, 143

1 Samuel
2:7—157
18:1, 3-4—244
25:37-38—160

2 Samuel
11:1-17—215
11:1-27—191

1 Kings
18:38—148
19:8—xv

Psalms
1:1-3—121, 268
1:2-3—117, 143

2:12—211
17:8—134
18:1-6—27
18:2—25, 28
19:14—129, 143
23:1-4—7, 13
23:1-6—37
32:8-9—206
32:1—215
32:1-2—214, 218
34:18—78
38:3-11—188, 189
38:17—160, 268
38:18—196
50:19-20—192
51:1-19—212, 217
55:12-14—155
55:20-21—155
56:13—267
59:7—160
71:1—210
81:12—242
103:11-12—203
119:11—117, 130, 143
119:70—118
119:92—118
119:98—135, 142, 268
119:114—134, 268
138:8—59
139:1-6—107
139:2—95
139:13-14—59
138:13-18—97
139:1-6—103
139:14—94

139:23-24—107
147:3—78

Proverbs
3:3-5—256
4:23, 25—122, 139
8:10—99
11:28—267
11:29—160
12:8—99
15:1—48
15:32—257, 261
16:18—69
17:17—237, 248
21:1, 9—259
23:3-5—256
23:6-7—103
27:5—249
27:5-17—261
27:6—237
27:17—259
28:13—196
28:14—230
28:26—248

Song of Solomon
8:6-7—242

Ecclesiastes
3:11—234

Isaiah
1:18—196
26:3—130, 136
38:17--203
40:29—xiii
40:29-31—77

289

Made in the USA
Columbia, SC
29 January 2020